Social Capital and the Role of LinkedIn to Form, Develop and Maintain Irish Entrepreneurial Business Networks

Social Capital and the Role of LinkedIn to Form, Develop and Maintain Irish Entrepreneurial Business Networks

By

Ted Vickey

CAMBRIDGE
SCHOLARS
PUBLISHING

Social Capital and the Role of LinkedIn to Form, Develop and Maintain
Irish Entrepreneurial Business Networks,
by Ted Vickey

This book first published 2011

Cambridge Scholars Publishing

12 Back Chapman Street, Newcastle upon Tyne, NE6 2XX, UK

British Library Cataloguing in Publication Data
A catalogue record for this book is available from the British Library

ISBN (10): 1-4438-2904-8, ISBN (13): 978-1-4438-2904-5

In memory of
Nancy O'Neill Vickey, 1943 – 2006
and Peter O'Neill, 1939- 2009

Special thanks to Dr. Michele O'Dwyer (University of Limerick) as Editor of this book and to Dr. Dennis Beck (University of Arkansas) and Tom Doyle Jr. for assistance in review of this book.

TABLE OF CONTENTS

ABSTRACT

The aim of this research is to investigate how Irish entrepreneurs use LinkedIn to form, develop and maintain a business network. The focus is to provide a descriptive account of social capital and entrepreneurship. Successful entrepreneurs understand the principles of business networking and how to improve wealth, health and happiness by creating rich social capital, tapping the hidden resources in their business, professional and personal networks.

This research starts with a review of the existing literature to create a foundation on social capital and entrepreneurship, then determines the perceived benefits of social networking. Finally, it concludes with an analysis of how Irish entrepreneurs use technology to increase their social capital.

This research will provide insight on three research questions:

- What are the perceived benefits of networking?
- How do Irish entrepreneurs form, maintain and develop an entrepreneurial network?
- What is the use of technology to manage social capital?

This research explores these questions through semi-structured interviews with ten Irish entrepreneurs. Results showed an unexpected lack of technology to form, develop and maintain a business network. They also provide insight of the diffusion of technology into Irish social capital. Ireland remains a nation based on the principle of face to face business interactions.

CHAPTER ONE

INTRODUCTION

This research presents a qualitative analysis of how Irish entrepreneurs use technology, such as LinkedIn, in the formation, development and maintenance of professional business networks and in so doing manage social capital. The research explores how entrepreneurs in Ireland perceive social networking services and how a select sample of Irish entrepreneurs employ LinkedIn as a professional networking tool. As such, the research explores how entrepreneurs manage their professional network through LinkedIn and examines the possible implications of such use.

Research has shown that interpersonal communication is one of the most important reasons why people use the Internet (Olsen, 2008). Since 2001 there has been a rapid expansion of what is described as social network services that focus on interaction between members (Boyd and Ellison, 2007). Professional networking and the subsequent use of social capital has become an important aspect of business for many entrepreneurs.

At the time of this research, several social networking services were available as a business tool to provide support to the formation, development and maintenance of professional networks. No longer is an entrepreneur limited by geographical location. Online social networking services have eliminated the four walls of brick and mortar found in traditional networking and now provide global access in real time to entrepreneurs regardless of industry.

1.1 LinkedIn as a social networking service

LinkedIn is an interconnected network of experienced professionals from around the world. Members of the network can find, be introduced to, and collaborate with, qualified professionals needed to accomplish both personal and professional goals (LinkedIn, 2009). LinkedIn's focus remains on networking, but extra features allow members to do so in a faster, more efficient and more productive manner. A member can add a profile, join groups of common interest, share advice with other entrepreneurs and start discussions. Time spent on LinkedIn has grown by 70% as the number of features has increased (Enterprise Ireland, 2009).

Created in 2003, LinkedIn has grown to a social network of over 90 million as of January 2011, 40 million in the U.S. and 50 million internationally representing 170 industries in 200 countries. A new member joins LinkedIn approximately every second, with available languages currently in English, French, German, Italian, Portuguese and Spanish. LinkedIn now has over 1,000 full-time employees around the world (LinkedIn, 2011). In the company's 2011 Securities and Exchange Commission filing for an initial public offering, LinkedIn disclosed that it was able to double its 2009 revenues to $161.4 million in the first nine months of 2010, with revenue from three products: hiring solutions (job listings), marketing solutions (advertising) and premium subscriptions.

LinkedIn reached profitability in March 2006 due to the LinkedIn premium service. According to Business Week, "LinkedIn's audience demographics are gold-plated. The average user is 41 and has a household income of $109,000. A $53 million dollar purchase of 5% of the company, by Venture Capital firms Bain Capital, Sequoia, Greylock Partners and Bessemer, gave LinkedIn a $1 billion dollar valuation and it continues to grow" (Enterprise Ireland website, 2009).

LinkedIn usage by professionals in Ireland is still in its infancy with an estimated 118,000 Irish members currently a part of the site. However, Irish membership has increased by 15% since July 2009 (Enterprise Ireland, 2009).

1.2 Research Issue

When entrepreneurs search for important information such as career opportunities, new ventures or expertise requests, it has become commonplace to contact a professional network for assistance (Olsen, 2008). The concept of gaining access to resources through friends or acquaintances is far from new (Ancona and Caldwell, 1988) and has become a frequent element to many businesses.

Many professionals also build and maintain professional networks intentionally as a way of doing business (Nardi et al., 2002). Traditional networking has included the exchange of business cards at conferences or meetings with follow-up emails or telephone calls. For many years, tools such as Microsoft Outlook have tracked the demographic information of a network, but the effort to ensure that the previously collected information was current was time consuming and thus often ignored. Social networking services, such as LinkedIn, have been created to provide an all-in-one application that makes the maintenance and development of a network as easy as sending an email. Because of the individual needs of an entrepreneur, LinkedIn may not replace an entire suite of applications, but it has been proven a strong complement with regard to professional networking.

In order to understand how LinkedIn is used by Irish entrepreneurs it is important to gain insight into what a social network is and how social networks are supported through the Internet. It is also beneficial to acquire knowledge about the elements that build social networks and how these building-blocks correlate to business success (Olsen, 2008). As such, this research will provide a general overview of social networks by describing how the networks are formed, developed and maintained using technology within a social space. This research on Irish entrepreneurs and the use of technology to form, maintain and develop social capital through business networking was based on a similar Norwegian research project (Olsen, 2008).

1.3 Research objectives

This research explores a number of issues in relation to Irish entrepreneurs and the use of technology on networking practices. The objectives of the research are as follows:

- Ascertain the perceived benefits of networking by Irish entrepreneurs;
- Explore how Irish entrepreneurs form, maintain and develop their network and
- Explore how Irish entrepreneurs use technology to manage social capital.

1.4 Research methodology

The research methodology for this study is qualitative and consists of semi-structured interviews with Irish entrepreneurs. Qualitative research was chosen for this study as qualitative methods are used to examine an individual's experience or behaviour, or to undertake a research issue which is exploratory and aims to discover information on a relatively new topic (Ghauri and Gronhaug, 2005).

CHAPTER TWO

LITERATURE REVIEW

2.1 Introduction

Chapter Two explores the foundational literature on areas pertinent to this research including entrepreneurship, business networking, social capital and social networking services. Following an extensive review of literature, a conceptual framework for this research is presented in this chapter. The literature review provides the foundation from which the conceptual model will be built.

2.2 Defining entrepreneurship

Before analysing literature on social networking, it is necessary to first review the research with regards to the definition of 'entrepreneurship'. The word entrepreneurship derives from the French words 'entre', meaning between and 'prendre', meaning to take. The word was originally used to describe people who "take on the risk" between buyers and sellers or who take on a task such as starting a new venture (Barringer, 2008). A number of theorists have defined entrepreneurship in a variety of ways. Schumpeter (1947, 1949) believed that the function of the entrepreneur was to exploit an innovation. In contrast, Kirzner (1973) believed that an entrepreneur could identify an opportunity in order to make a profit rather than creating an opportunity. Carton et al. (1998, p. 1) definition of entrepreneurship combines definitions from theorists like Schumpeter (1947) into an all-inclusive and satisfactory concept:

> "Entrepreneurship is the pursuit of a discontinuous opportunity involving the creation of an organization (or sub-organization) with the expectation of value creation to the participants. The entrepreneur is the individual (or team) that identifies the opportunity, gathers the necessary resources, creates and is ultimately responsible for the performance of the organization. Therefore, entrepreneurship is the means by which new organizations are formed with their resultant job and wealth creation."

Entrepreneurs are generally described as innovative, creative individuals who are determined, have a self-belief and are calculated risk takers (O'Gorman, 1997). However, entrepreneurs are also the managers of their ventures and must exhibit management skills; routine management of a venture is not synonymous with entrepreneurship (Dana, 2001). According to the Global Entrepreneurship Monitor study in 2005, about 330 million or roughly 14% of adults in the nations surveyed are involved with forming new businesses (Barringer, 2008). The same study indicates that firms that grow to over 20 employees are responsible for 80% of all new jobs worldwide.

Entrepreneurship is critical for every economy as it generates wealth and reduces unemployment (Dana, 2001). Entrepreneurs improve the economic growth of a country and therefore governments dedicate a lot of time and money to policies and incentives that encourage it (Dana, 2001).

As entrepreneurs pursue opportunities without regard to resources of control, it is essential that the entrepreneur connects with different stakeholders such as suppliers, wholesalers, agents and financial institutions/investors (Olsen, 2008). By engaging with these different stakeholders, entrepreneurs can source valuable information that would otherwise be unavailable (Dana, 2001). It is through this connection with other entrepreneurs that an effective network is built that facilitates the running of business; this 'linking together' of business people is called 'networking' (Blundel, 2001).

2.2.1 Defining the concept of networking in business

In order to establish the importance of networking for entrepreneurial businesses, it is necessary to initially establish what is meant by the term 'network' and the process of engaging in 'networking'. The following statements are some of the definitions of the term 'business network' which have been advanced by research experts in this field:

Rosenfield, 1997, p. 3	"A group of firms with restricted membership and specific, and often contractual, business objectives likely to result in mutual financial gains. The members of a network choose each other, for a variety of reasons; they agree explicitly to co-operate in some way and to depend on each other to some extent."
Blundel and Smith, 2001, p. 1	"A complex pattern of formal and informal linkages between individuals, businesses and other organizations such as government and voluntary agencies."
Ffowcs-Williams et al., 2003, p. 13	"...group of firms using their combined talents and resources to co-operate on joint development projects. Through complementing each other and specializing in order to overcome common problems, participants are able to achieve collective efficiency and conquer markets beyond their individual reach."
Bergman and Feser, 2000, p. 1	"...groupings of companies directly concerned with the conduct of some form of business activity."

Table 2.1: Definitions of Business Network

Business networking may be inter-organizational and may also be facilitated by trade associations. Chambers of Commerce, professional bodies and public sector agencies (Bergman, 2000) are all examples of trade associations. Those organizations that vigorously facilitate networking generally do so within the context of a broader support service to companies and are typically membership-based organizations that are structured along local, regional, national or professional occupation lines (Bergman, 2000). Companies perceive networks as being a valuable asset (Hunt et al., 2006).

Lynch et al. (2009) suggests that 'business networking' is not an end in itself but rather a means to enhancing business performance and efficiency. Furthermore, the logic model they presented allows the properties and dynamics of business networking to be understood as an important and necessary component of the economy (Lynch et al., 2009).

Networks may be formal "hard" networks involving firms joining together specifically to co-market, co-produce or co-operate in product or market development (Bergman and Feser, 2000). Networks can also be informal "soft" networks involving firms joining together in an effort to solve common problems, share information, acquire new skills or jointly provide training (Bergman, 2000).

Networking can also be defined as the process of establishing and preserving interpersonal relationships, which are directed by principles of expectations and obligations (Coleman, 1990). This view is shared by Williams (2000) who sees networking as a long-term process which is based on genuine trust and reciprocity of relationships. By forming these relationships and being part of a network one has access to information, resources, support and guidance (Knouse and Webb, 2001).

Hunt et al. (2006, p. 4) describe why networks are important to businesses:

> "Networks help firms to achieve critical mass and economies of scale and compete in larger, more diverse and more competitive markets than they could if they were to continue to act alone. By concentrating on core competencies and creating a network of specialized suppliers and partners, firms can develop their unique assets, stay flexible and adaptable and at the same time be able to respond to the demands of the global market."

Nardi et al. (2002) suggest a three-phase approach that networkers need to achieve to create a successful professional network, which include: building a network, maintaining the network and activating selected contacts. In addition, Olsen (2008) stresses that networkers need to continue to add new contacts to their network in order to access as many resources as possible, and to maintain their network through staying in touch with their contacts (Olsen, 2008).

2.2.2 Access to networks and level of networking

Ffowcs-Williams (2003) found that it is easier for large businesses to form a network than for entrepreneurial firms, and that networks take much longer to form than is often expected. This research also found that it is often difficult for government agencies to encourage entrepreneurs to participate in their networking programs and that information which is given to owner/managers at meetings has a greater impact than written information (Ffowcs-Williams, 2003). Researchers have debated the level of networking in which a small entrepreneurial firm engages. According to Birley (1991) it is highly possible that small business owners have a larger network than those in employment, while Curren (1993) suggests that networking is virtually impossible for the small business owner due to time constraints and due to the fact that entrepreneurs are independent by nature. O'Donnell's (2004) study supported this and believes that owner/managers see the involvement in networking as "antithetical" to entrepreneurial culture. This is supported by Devin (1989) and Burns and Dewhurst (1996) who believe that entrepreneurs tend not to participate in networking due to their psychological characteristics. However, Dollinger (1985) suggests that the stereotype of the entrepreneur as a 'lone ranger' is a flawed image. Crommie (1994) supports this view and found networking to be important in small firms, whereby the owner/manager of the firm depends significantly on the support of a lot of people.

Despite the myth of individualism, social capital is an essential part of achieving personal success, business success, and even a happy and satisfying life.

> "The source of success is natural talent, intelligence, education, or effort. It might even be sheer luck. Success is an individual matter. Every person succeeds or fails on the basis of his or her own individual efforts and abilities." (Baker, 2000, p. 3)

To suggest that fate depends on relationships often runs counter to the belief system of entrepreneurs: individualism. Individualism is a key trait to the entrepreneurial culture that teaches and celebrates independence, self-reliance, self-sufficiency, self-interest and self-determination. Baker (2000, p.4) suggests this:

> "Individualism is a myth. The myth is that society consists of independent individuals, who act to achieve goals that are independently arrived at. This fiction gets in the way of understanding how the world actually works. The myth lowers our chances of success, depresses our pay, limits our promotions, decreases the value we create, reduces our ability to get things done, and even jeopardizes our health, happiness, welfare and most importantly closes off all the great possibilities of life. By understanding the role of relationships, however, we can tap hidden resources that will enable us to be much more successful in all areas of our lives—work, family and community."

Baker (2000) is not alone in an evaluation of entrepreneurial individualism. Other authors suggest the following:

Fraser and Dutta (2008)	"Humans are social creatures who are restless in their pursuit of the satisfactions, reassurances and benefits procured by competitive advantages, conferred status and material gain. For most of us, these goals can only be achieved socially through personal connections with other people. In short, through linkages we create contacts, connections, complicity, collaboration and conspiracies – which we are constantly creating, expanding and maintaining with those around us."
Huggins (2000)	"Individuals who are 'well connected', that is who have a large number of social and professional relationships, will experience more success in starting new ventures due to the existence of the large rich network."
DeCarolis et al. (2009)	"We further postulate that the information and resources embedded in these networks are valuable to the formation and progression of new ventures. Networks facilitate access to critical resources, such as suppliers (e.g., manufacturers, marketers, venture capitalists, universities and attorneys), employees and customers."

Table 2.2: Evaluation of entrepreneurial individualism

It is often suggested that entrepreneurs must network in order to survive (Huggins, 2000). Ferrazzi (2005) goes so far as to state that "the dynamics are the same whether you are working at a corporation or attending a society event – 'invisibility' is a fate worse than failure." Both points suggest the growing importance of successful networking for an entrepreneur and that failure to do so can at times create negative consequences for those that either can't or won't network.

2.2.3 Proactive versus reactive networking

Researchers have also researched whether or not small business networking is proactive or reactive; with Curran et al. (1993) stating that small business networking has many limitations and is generally a proactive process, and that small business owners do not consciously plan their networking activity (McGowan and Rocks, 1995). Other research contrasts this view by suggesting that networking can be both planned and subconscious. Aldrich and Zimmer (1986) found that social relations are to varying degrees purposeful, as some may arise accidentally or may occur through a chance encounter with an individual, while others may occur due to deliberate planned interactions in order to obtain specific information. Shaw (1997) found evidence that subjects of the study noted the advantages for their business as being part of specific networks and that the subjects often deliberately set out 'to network'.

2.2.3.1 Small firm networking

One reason why there is confusion as to whether or not small to medium enterprises (SME) engage in networking activities is that much of the research conducted thus far on networking in SMEs has been quantitative in nature and has not been able to establish how owner/managers of SMEs actually interact with other members of the network (O'Donnell and Cummins, 1999). O'Donnell and Cummins (1999) found that owner/managers network in order to obtain two things: information on their competitors and on developments in their industry as a whole.

Research suggests that networking was most productive at social events and that there was a high degree of co-operation amongst competitors (O'Donnell and Cummins, 1999). Another important reason identified by the research for networking was to maintain a good relationship with customers (O'Donnell and Cummins, 1999). Networking was also recognized as a necessary activity when a firm entered into a new market (O'Donnell and Cummins, 1999). Networking was seen as a deliberate action by the networker, yet the most productive networking seemed to occur when it was unplanned and opportunistic by nature (O'Donnell and Cummins, 1999). Although the practice of networking was seen as 'a means to an end' that had to result in a tangible outcome, it was an activity in which the networkers saw as beneficial and something which the networker aimed to develop and improve upon (O'Donnell and Cummins, 1999).

2.2.4 Networking analysis

Lynch et al. (2009) provides a brief history of networking analysis by describing Marshall's (1895) appreciation of the advantages of firm cooperation and Coase's (1937) observation that no single firm possesses the capabilities to complete every business activity necessary for growth. Each business network is unique, varying in the scope and structure of the network, whether the network is formal or informal, and whether the network is designed for social networking or for inter-firm networking (Lynch et al., 2009).

Positive reinforcement from early success in a network contributes to the likelihood of long-term success of the network. Thus, business owners should set attainable goals at the onset and continue to inform other members of the network of any subsequent success (Hunt et al., 2006). In addition, regular interaction among network members in the beginning of the network is crucial to network success and that "only those companies that have a winning formula of costs, quality, capability, innovativeness and price will be able to compete successfully" (Hunt et al., 2006).

Networking give firms the advantage of sharing costs and risks that would otherwise be too high to take on alone. In addition, networking also contains less obvious advantages. Research suggests that contact between different firms (e.g., managers and staff members) increases the amount of knowledge contained within a given firm (Hunt et al., 2006). This increased knowledge is known as 'networked learning' and is quickly becoming valuable in the professional world (Hunt et al., 2006).

Although networks can be particularly advantageous to businesses, there are also specific disadvantages and risks associated with networking. Lynch et al. (2009) suggests that many business owners are concerned with the risk of sharing information with another business. Business owners may be hesitant to network with another business for fear of becoming "locked into" an unproductive business relationship, or for fear of an unbalanced relationship (e.g., one partner may contribute more than the other partner, resulting in a "free rider" situation). Thus, maintaining network relationships largely depends on cultivating a strong sense of trust within a network.

However, networking also fosters competitiveness, thereby motivating innovation and enhancing growth. Hunt et al. (2006) points out that businesses that are best able to incorporate new research and technologies are the most productive and successful. Thus, networking enables companies to learn more quickly and to adapt faster.

In summation, business networking is a three phase process which includes building a network, maintaining the network and activating selected contacts (Nardi et al., 2002). While there remains a divide in the research regarding the importance of networking for entrepreneurs, their business success depends significantly on the support of a lot of people (Cromie, 1994).

Figure 2.1 illustrates business networking as the first of four concepts for the conceptual model.

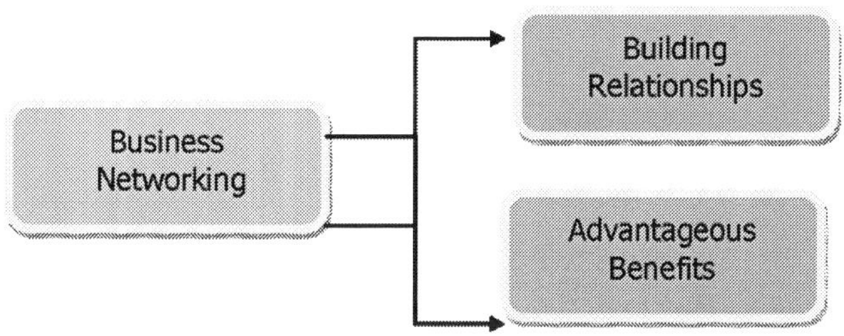

Figure 2.1: Business networking as first foundation in conceptual model

2.3 Networking in Ireland

Formal networking between firms has gained popularity in Ireland over the past few years. The actual number of individual networks between Irish entrepreneurs is difficult to calculate. However, Hunt et al. (2006) estimated that there are approximately 110 formalised networks and clusters in Ireland with the formation of networks to be a current phenomenon, as most of the networks identified had been established within the five years prior to the study.

Lynch et al. (2009) points out that numerous resources have been allocated to Irish networking policies. For example, the Irish government devoted €20 million per annum for five years to support the creation of enterprise-led networks (Lynch et al., 2009). One of Ireland's most recent networking strategies, the Pilot Initiative for Collaborative Projects, was presented by Ireland's Enterprise Strategy Group (Lynch et al., 2009). The initiative was intended to "establish the potential of industry-led networks to act as a catalyst in attaining enterprise and economic success in Ireland" (Lynch et al., 2009, p. 167).

As both globalization and networking have begun to play an increasingly important role across Ireland, researchers have spent increased effort understanding the exact nature of this role. "However, little is known about the extent of business networks across the island." (Hunt et al., 2006 p. 3) Although there has long been recognition of networking policy interventions in countries such as Ireland, Spain and the UK, little research has sought to examine these interventions (Lynch et al., 2009).

Ironically, with the increase of globalization, companies have come to depend on collaboration. With market expansion and complexity, companies less able to retain the skills and expertise in-house that are required for competitive success must look elsewhere for the needed expertise. As a result, collaboration is a critical component of economic success. In fact, "economists and economic geographers have long highlighted the importance of dense collaborative networks of businesses to the economic success of regions" (Hunt et al., 2006, p. 3).

Hunt et al. (2006) made the recommendation of raising the awareness of the benefits that can be reaped from networks as a method to increase the number of networks present in Ireland. Historically, networks have played an important role in development throughout Ireland. Even though networks continue to play an important role, their presence has gone unrecorded (Hunt et al., 2006).

2.4 Defining social capital

The term social capital has been reinvented at least six times throughout the twentieth century, each time to call attention to the ways in which our lives are made more productive by social ties (Anderson, 2002). The nature of social capital can be seen as a bi-polar puzzle in that it is said to be both glue, which forms the structure of networks, and simultaneously a lubricant that facilitates the operation of networks (Anderson, 2002). Analysis of social capital continued through the end of the century with a greater importance of social relationships in business activity (Anderson, 2002) and a focus on interaction between members (Boyd, 2007).

Social capital refers to the many resources available in both personal and business networks (Baker, 2000). These resources include information, ideas, leads, business opportunities, financial capital, power, emotional support, goodwill, trust and cooperation (Baker, 2000). Even natural talent, intelligence, education, effort and luck are not individual attributes at all; these skills are developed, shaped, and expressed by and through relationships with others, thus important aspects to social capital (Baker,

2000). The difficulties of defining social capital stem from the confusion in the literature and demonstrate the problems of defining social capital as an asset (Cope, 2007). Researchers view social capital as a condition or a quality that revolves around the experience of interdependence. It is 'a social thing' linked to the social interactions within a network. (Cope, 2007).

Others define social capital as the goodwill created through social relations that can be mobilized to facilitate the attainment of needed resources, influence and sponsorship (Adler and Kwon, 2002). Social capital is embedded in relationships that facilitate collaboration and cooperation to achieve mutual benefits that include feelings of gratitude, reciprocity, respect and friendship (De Carolis, 2009). The role of social capital in entrepreneurship research has demonstrated the impact of social interaction on information flow and innovation in the hi-tech sector while showing that entrepreneurship is inseparable from social interaction (Cope, 2007).

Although research has provided useful descriptions of the importance of social capital, there remain a number of different definitions for the term. For example, Anderson and Jack (2002, p. 207) suggested that social capital is not a 'thing' but a process:

> "It is the process of creating a condition for the effective exchange of information and resources. It can only exist between people; accordingly it is a relational artefact which we can only observe as one or other of its dimensional manifestations. From this perspective, social capital can be envisioned as a bridge building process linking individuals, so that networks are a series of bridges that links a number of individuals."

Other definitions are as follows:

Social Capital…	
… is the goodwill that is engendered by the fabric of social relations and that can be mobilized to facilitate action.	(Adler, 2002, p. 2)
… includes many aspects of the social context, such as social interaction, social ties, trusting relationships and value systems that facilitate the actions of individuals located in a particular social context.	(Nahapiet, 1997, p. 17; Tsai, 1998, p. 18)
… is said to be both the origin and the expression of successful network interactions.	(Cooke, 1999, p. 19)
… is increasingly recognized that interpersonal relationships have a crucial role to play in the success of individuals.	(Coleman, 1988; Putnam et al., 1993)
… might be described as the operation of a social process, where non co-operative action would lead to a reduction in information and resources flows. In contrast an interaction within a rich endowment of social capital is likely to enhance information and resource flows. Furthermore, the possession of social capital may reduce transaction costs.	(Putnam et al., 1993)
… reduces transaction costs because of untraded interdependencies.	(Dosi, 1988)
Though we spend the vast majority of our lives developing our technical capabilities to make us attractive in the job market, few of us put specific focus on developing our people skills. But it is the people skills – also known as social capital – that determines our overall success.	(Dittmer, 2008, p. 25)

Table 2.3: Definitions of social capital

In summation, social capital is the origin and the expression of successful network interactions (Cooke, 1999). Although not a recent area of business, new research into social capital shows the importance of not only understanding what social capital is, but also how entrepreneurs can use their social capital to grow their business. Figure 2.2 illustrates Social Capital as the second of four foundations for the conceptual model.

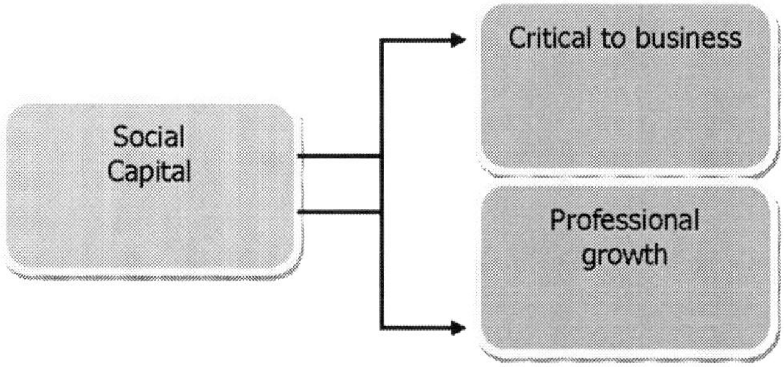

Figure 2.2: Social Capital as second foundation of conceptual model

2.5 Understanding social networking in a business environment

A social network is built on the same principles as any other network. To better understand the concept of a social capital network, the social capital network can be compared to a computer network - whereas a computer network has computers and wires, a personal network has actors and relations (Garton, 1997). In relation to a social network, the actors represent individuals while the ties represent the relations between them. If an actor has a set of ties, he/she has a social network (Garton, 1997). A social network is often described as a dynamic system that varies according to time and circumstances, something which makes it flexible according to size, strength and situation (Haythornthwaite, 2000). A person may, for example, decrease or increase communications within existing ties and/or lose or gain contact with actors. A social network is also a group of people that have a certain pattern of contact or interaction. The pattern, or tie, may be that of friendship between individuals, business relationships between companies, geographical proximity or a professional acquaintance.

2.6 Motivations for creation of social network

Individuals are motivated to join social networking sites for a variety of complex reasons. Fraser and Dutta (2008) organise these motivations into two categories: rational motivation and nonrational motivation. Rational motivation defines individuals who join social networking sites for a specific intent and calculations. For example, professionals who join sites related to career development, such as LinkedIn, do so as a result of rational calculations. In comparison, young adults who join sites such as Facebook and MySpace in order to connect to friends do so as a result of their instinct to forge social bonds, and thus possess nonrational motivations.

Networks have been identified as important to firm growth, mitigating the liability of newness, providing legitimacy and preventing failure. Networks connect the entrepreneur with opportunities critical to a firm's success, facilitate innovation, spread risks and provide support, credibility and contact for entrepreneurs (DeCarolis et al., 2009).

Because of the many elements that build a person's social network, it will usually be quite complex (Haythornthwaite, 2000). The social network will probably consist of both weak and strong ties that are intertwined in a number of ways and, in addition, each tie may consist of several multiplex connections of their own. In other words, the connections within a social network might vary from weak acquaintances to strong friendships depending on the tie and the actors' desire to connect with each other (Haythornthwaite, 2000).

With regard to business and entrepreneurship, social capital becomes the keystone of success for relationships available in and through personal and business networks. If human capital is what is known (knowledge, skills and experience), then access to social capital depends on who is known (size, quality and diversity of your network) and who isn't known but directly connected to via a network (Baker, 2000).

Baker (2000, p. 1) defines the importance of social capital within the scope of business practice:

> "These resources include information, ideas, leads, business opportunities, financial capital, power and influence, emotional support, even goodwill, trust and cooperation. The "social" in social capital emphasizes that these resources are not personal assets; no single person owns them."

Baker (2000) also provides additional insight into social capital by comparing social capital to human capital or financial capital, where the capital is productive, enabling users to create value, get things done, achieve goals, fulfil missions in life and make contributions to the world. Baker also suggests that the importance in the productive nature of social capital can often be understated:

> "No one can be successful — or even survive — without it. But many people believe they should be able to get along without social capital; they mistake "going it alone" as the prescription for success. Others pretend to thrive without social capital, using it secretly as if it were improper or even unethical. These beliefs and attitudes are rooted in the myth of

> individualism: the cultural belief that everyone succeeds or fails on the basis of individual efforts and abilities." (Baker, 2000, p.2)

Many professionals also build and maintain professional networks intentionally as a way of doing business (Nardi et al., 2002). Professional networking has become a valuable asset to businesses in general and an important aspect of many professionals' work and growth (Olsen, 2008).

2.7 Reciprocity of social capital

Networks involve almost by definition mutual obligations; those within the network are not interested as being a mere 'contact' (Putnam, 2000). Networks of community engagement foster sturdy norms of reciprocity: 'I'll do this for you now, in the expectation that you (or perhaps someone else) will return the favour' (Putnam, 2000).

In some cases, reciprocity is specific: 'I'll do this for you if you do that for me' (Putnam, 2000). Related is the norm of generalized reciprocity: 'I'll do this for you without expecting anything from you in return with the confident expectation that someone else will eventually do something for me' (Putnam, 2000). The Golden Rule is one formulation of generalized reciprocity (Putnam, 2000).

Similarly, Fraser and Dutta (2008) suggest that networks become more socially useful as the number of members in that network increase. This idea is known as Metcalfe's Law, named after Ethernet inventor Robert Metcalfe. The maxim suggests that "the value of a network is proportional to the square of the number of people it connects (Fraser and Dutta, 2008, p. 67).

In addition:

> "Metcalfe noted from an economic perspective that after a certain critical mass of network connectivity is reached, the network's benefits grow more than its costs. Metcalfe's Law was modified by David Reed who suggested that the law underestimated the utility value of network growth. Reed suggested that the utility of a network grows exponentially with its size." (Fraser and Dutta, 2008, p. 67)

A relationship can also be directed or undirected (Garton, 1997); for example, a directed relationship is one where one person may give support to a second person. This example highlights two directed relationships: the giving of support and the receiving of support (Garton, 1997). Alternately, actors may share an undirected friendship relationship, i.e., both maintain the relationship and there is no specific direction to it (Garton, 1997). However, while two individuals may both share friendship, the relationship may be unbalanced: one actor may claim a close friendship while the other a weaker friendship, or communication may be initiated more frequently by one actor than the other (Garton, 1997). Thus, although the relationship is shared, its expression may be asymmetrical (Garton, 1997).

2.8 Entrepreneurial leverage of social capital

Walker and Gubbins (2007) identified three theories borrowed from sociology to highlight how entrepreneurs can leverage social capital to add value to their firms.

> "First, Burt's (1992) theory of structural holes combines with Granovetter's (1973) theory of weak ties to suggest that entrepreneurs can add value because they change the social relationships that 'bridge' different people or groups to one another. Second, Coleman's (1988) and Putnam's (1995) closure theories suggest that entrepreneurs can add value because they change the social relationships that bond people together in groups. Third and finally, Lin's (2001) theory of social structure and action suggests that entrepreneurs can add value because 'more' or 'different' resources are exchanged."

Not only does social capital and networking bridge people together, it also creates value for those who are active in their participation not by the actual participation but also the ability to share between both bridges and bonds.

In organizational studies, the concept of social capital is gaining popularity. Social capital proves to be a powerful factor explaining relative success in a number of arenas of central concern to business researchers:

Social Capital …

… influences career success	(Burr, 1992; Gabbay and Zuckerman, 1998; Podolny and Baron, 1997)
… influences executive compensation	(Belliveau, O'Reilly and Wade, 1996; Burt, 1997a)
… helps workers find jobs	(Granovetter, 1973, 1995; Lin and Dumin, 1996; Lin, Ensel and Vaughn, 1981)
… creates a richer pool of recruits for firms	(Fernandez, Castilla and Moore, 2000)
… facilitates inter-company resource exchange and product innovation	(Gabbay and Zuckerman, 1998; Hansen, 1998; Tsai and Ghoshal, 1998)
… increases the creation of intellectual capital	(Hargadon and Sutton, 1997; Nahapiet and Ghoshal, 1998)
… decreases staff turnover and organizational dissolution rates	(Krackhardt and Hanson, 1993
… facilitates entrepreneurship	(Chong and Gibbons, 1997)
… facilitates in formation of start-up companies	(Walker, Kogut and Shan, 1997)
… strengthens supplier relations	(Asanuma, 1985; Baker, 1990; Dore, 1983; Gerlach, 1992; Helper, 1990)
… strengthens regional production networks	(Romo and Schwartz, 1995)
… increases and inter-firm learning	(Kraatz, 1998)

Figure 2.3: Benefits of Social Capital

The majority of individuals is embedded in social situations and consequently take advantage of the wider social relations in which ties are already embedded (Kim and Aldrich, 2005). A recent survey of the application and meaning of social capital confirmed that by making connections with others with shared values, individuals are able to achieve more than if acting alone (Field, 2003).

2.9 Network tie strength

Social capital can be described as a bridge-building process linking individuals so that networks are a series of bridges that link numerous individuals (Anderson, 2002). This description would explain the structural element of social capital; the constructing of bridges (Anderson, 2002). The bridges of social capital link two individuals but with ranges of carrying capacity (Anderson, 2002):

> "...building a social capital bridge is not simply a linking of individuals but the strength of the bridge's construction serves as an indicator of the amount of traffic-carrying capability. So, a robust social capital bridge will allow better access to a richer range of resources and information. Moreover, if a bridge is to be built quickly it is required to be built from each side of the gap. This captures the essence of mutuality in social capital". (Anderson and Jack, 2002, p. 207)

A professional network generally consists of a combination of strong and weak ties that are activated when the individual is in need of resources on a professional level (Nardi et al., 2002). The professional network is primarily built with the intention of supplying this need (Nardi et al., 2002). As a result, professional networks are generally more ego-centred than personal networks (Nardi et al., 2002).

In general, a network tie is considered as strong when there is an emotional exchange of information such as social support, advice and/or confidence (Olsen, 2008). People who are connected through strong ties will usually share resources, meet face-to-face and help each other with personal problems (Olsen, 2008). A tie is considered weak when there is a low level of intimacy and little exchange of personal information, often bound through work, school or geographical proximity (Garton, 1997).

Research studies have suggested that an individual's personal network is most often a combination of strong and weak ties that are primarily oriented towards a personal motive during the exchange of resources (Haythornthwaite, 2000). Social support, companionship, emotional aid and advice are typical exchanges within a personal network (Haythornthwaite, 2000).

The strong tie/weak tie theory suggests that our acquaintances (weak ties) are less likely to be socially involved with one another than are our close friends (strong ties) (Granovetter, 1973). Thus, the set of people made up of any individual and acquaintances comprises a low-density network (one in which many of the possible relational lines are absent), whereas the set consisting of the same individual and close friends will be densely knit (many of the possible lines are present) (Granovetter, 1973).

> "...an individual will have a collection of close friends, most of who are in touch with one another--a densely knit clump of social structure. The individual will also have a collection of acquaintances, few of whom know one another. Each of these acquaintances, however, is likely to have close friends in a closely knit clump of social structure, but one different from the original individual. The weak tie between the individual and their acquaintance, therefore, becomes not merely a trivial acquaintance tie but rather a crucial bridge between the two densely knit clumps of close friends." (Granovetter, 1973, p. 202)

Granovetter (1973, p.1) suggested: "... the strength of a tie is a (probably linear) combination of the amount of time, the emotional intensity, the intimacy (mutual confiding) and the reciprocal services which characterize the tie." Prior to this study most sociologists had focused on strong ties, giving weak ties little or no importance in relation to a person's social network (Olsen, 2008). Granovetter (1973) argued, however, that weak ties definitely had their strengths, especially as bridges between small-scale interaction and large-scale patterns (Olsen, 2008).

Granovetter (1973) also compared weak ties to bridges, the only path connecting two points that in so doing provides a route of resources between people (Olsen, 2008). Though all weak ties may not function as bridges, according to Granovetter (1973), with very few exceptions all bridges are weak ties (Olsen, 2008). In addition, Granovetter (1973) suggested that each tie not only provides direct access between individuals, but also indirectly to each other's connections and thus it is the weak ties that provide the opportunity to connect with new individuals (Olsen, 2008). Because of this fact, the potential of a weak tie in terms of relationship building can be monumental (Olsen, 2008). Thus, the loss of a weak tie could do more damage to a person's social network than the loss of a strong tie (Olsen, 2008). The removal of a strong tie may result in the loss of a confidant, but it will usually not result in the loss of many other ties within one's network (Olsen, 2008). Since more people can potentially be connected via weak ties, the loss of a weak tie will result in the loss of future connections through the existing connection (Granovetter, 1973).

Olsen (2008) suggests that the Internet might decrease the number of weak ties based on the assumption that the Internet makes it easier to communicate and connect with people from anywhere in the world. However, other researchers suggest instead that Internet sites, specifically social network sites, "have leveraged the strength of weak tie e-quaintances around specific consumer needs" (Fraser and Dutta, 2008, p. 57). Fraser and Dutta (2008) point out that sites that were initially consumer sites, particularly those in the travel and hotel industries, were among the first to accumulate and attract potential customers as e-quaintances.

In summation, with regard to business and entrepreneurship, social capital becomes the keystone of success for relationships available in and through personal and business networks. Networks are more than just connections between two individuals; networks establish a relationship that is based upon mutual obligations (Putnam, 2000). It is through the obliged relationships that entrepreneurial firms can grow as a business, as the relationships allow the firm to focus on the client. This ability to focus on the client is paramount for business success as it is cheaper and easier for a firm to maintain existing clients than to acquire new ones.

2.10 Social networking as an entrepreneurial activity

Relationships clearly matter to entrepreneurs, but understanding how these relationships function requires a true appreciation of social capital. The presence or absence of social capital is likely to influence the very nature of the entrepreneurial venture (Anderson and Miller, 2002). Social capital involves social interaction and would appear to reside in and between connections to others. Social capital could even be regarded as representing 'networking capital' since in essence it is really a relational phenomenon and a term that actually refers to the social connections entrepreneurs use to obtain resources otherwise acquire through expending their human or financial capital (Aldrich and Martinez, 2001; Anderson and Jack, 2002; Kim and Aldrich, 2005). Access to social networks is exclusive rather than inclusive, based upon mutual trust and shared understanding (Cope, 2007).

While economics is often seen as highly individualistic, the economics of entrepreneurship is socially embedded. There exists a bridge between transaction cost theory and theories of entrepreneurship, business culture and information. The crucial dimension is the relationship between trust and transaction costs. One concern is related to building the kinds of networks that will improve the performance of business and hence the macro-economy. Network building is not static but rather a dynamic process. The form and capabilities of networks will therefore depend on the stage in the entrepreneurial process and the reputation of the entrepreneur (Cope et al., 2007).

Although the entrepreneurial benefits of social capital are becoming well established, understanding the specific social processes that may enhance the ability of the entrepreneur to recognize or exploit opportunities is fairly limited (Davidsson and Honig, 2003). Yet, if entrepreneurship is a socioeconomic process whereby economic actions are conditioned, if not at the very least influenced, by social relations then understanding the impact of the social context on the entrepreneur becomes increasingly important (Aldrich and Zimmer, 1986; Granovetter, 1985; Young, 1998).

In terms of the entrepreneurial context for social capital, Fafchamps and Minten (1999) argue that if network capital is essential for firm growth, then smart entrepreneurs must accumulate network capital in just the same way as to accumulate physical resources. It is their view that social capital is a necessary precursor to entrepreneurship (Fafchamps, 1999). Fafchamps and Minten (1999) dismiss the idea that a well-developed network is merely a by-product of entrepreneurship but rather that good entrepreneurs invest in social interaction.

Until relatively recently, the study of entrepreneurship focused primarily upon the individual entrepreneur. Analysis of traits and cognitive behaviour models were firmly individualistic (Bolton and Thompson, 2000; Brockhaus and Horowitz, 1986; Kets de Vries, 1977). However, since the 1980s the importance of the networks of entrepreneurs and thus their social contacts has been more widely recognized (Cope, 2007). The emerging perspective is that since economic activity is embedded in society, the innovative entrepreneur develops social capital through building networks which provide external sources of information, support, finance and expertise allowing mutual learning and boundary crossing (Cope, 2007).

2.11 Benefits of social networking for an entrepreneur

Entrepreneurship is a field of business that seeks to understand how opportunities to create something new (innovation) are discovered or created by individuals who then use various means to exploit or develop them, and in so doing can produce a wide range of outcomes (Baron and Shane, 2005). This perspective of entrepreneurship reflects the core of entrepreneurship research—the investigation into how and why opportunities are discovered and exploited (De Carolis, 2009). Entrepreneurship is significant on many levels, as evidenced not only in government and public policy initiatives that encourage new business development, but also within established organizations that actively encourage the development and pursuit of new opportunities (De Carolis, 2009).

As discussed in Section 2.4, social capital includes benefits and resources that include but are not limited to the sharing of information, ideas, leads, business opportunities, financial capital, power, emotional support, goodwill, trust and cooperation (Baker, 2000). Even natural talent, intelligence, education, effort and luck are not individual attributes at all; these skills are developed, shaped and expressed by and through relationships with others, thus important aspects to social capital (Baker, 2000).

Three benefits of social networking are discussed in this report: information sharing, new venture creation and future business opportunity.

2.11.1 Benefits of social networking: information sharing

In recent years, the entrepreneurship literature has highlighted the significance of social networks in the creation and sustaining of new ventures (Aldrich et al., 1987; Carsrud and Johnson, 1989; Huggins, 2000 as cited in Anderson and Jack, 2002). The social network approach has been used in two ways. First, to demonstrate that the personal network of the owner/manager of a new venture allows access to resources that are not possessed internally (Ostgaard and Birley, 1994 as cited in Anderson, 2002); and second, to illustrate the influence of social embeddedness and the associated dynamics of economic exchange (Portes and Sensenbrenner, 1993; Johannisson and Landstrom, 1997 as cited in Anderson, 2002).

While both perspectives help in the understanding of the contribution of social networks to entrepreneurship, they do so in very different ways. At one level social networks are perceived to be important because the social networks open up entrepreneurial possibilities, providing access to useful, reliable, exclusive, less redundant information (Bruderl and Preisendorfer, 1998 as cited in Anderson, 2002). However, at another level social networks provide a mechanism for enacting the environment (Johannisson, 1988; Weick, 1969, 1987 as cited in Anderson and Jack, 2002); in other words, re-create by embedding so that networks become the medium of exchange. According to Johannisson (2000), while management needs structure, entrepreneurship thrives on process, ambiguity and action rationality. This leads entrepreneurs to react to new realities while at the same time continuously growing their network (Johannisson, 2000).

2.11.2 Benefits of social networking: new venture creation

Research has pointed to the importance of networking and building social capital to the new venture creation process (De Carolis, 2009). In particular, it has been argued that new venture creation is the result of the interplay of entrepreneurs' social networks (De Carolis, 2009). As the presence of entrepreneurial opportunities in a network increase, the odds of entrepreneurial behaviour increase, but only if someone is inclined toward entrepreneurial behaviour (De Carolis, 2009).

An entrepreneur's networks are likely to be based on experience, which not only determines the range of contacts, but may also influence perceptions of opportunities and courses of action (Aldrich and Zimmer, 1986; Birley, 1985; Chell and Baines, 2000; Dubini and Aldrich, 1991; Johannison, 1998; Johannison et al., 2002; Lechner and Dowling, 2003).

2.11.3 Benefits of social networking: future business opportunities

Networks may begin as personal in nature but are likely over time to grow to include a range of contacts that far exceeds an individual's immediate family and close friends (Cope, 2007). Individual contacts alone, while reducing uncertainty, may become constraints on both the entrepreneur and the business unless reinforced by a wider external network (Cope, 2007). External networks frequently involve more formal contractual arrangements, including strategic alliances with other companies (Cope, 2007). These weak ties allow the individual to reach outside his or her immediate contacts to secure a wider range of information.

In summation, social networking has a number of benefits associated with entrepreneurial activity. For the purposes of this paper, the benefits of social networking have been identified as: information sharing, new venture creation and future business opportunities.

Figure 2.4 illustrates the effects of social capital combined with entrepreneurship.

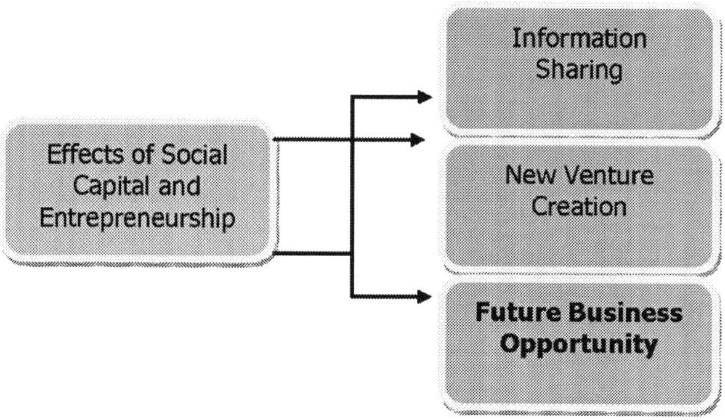

Figure 2.4: Social capital and entrepreneurship as the third foundation for the conceptual model

2.12 Technology Based Networking

Online social networking sites have found their place in our society (Fraser and Dutta, 2008). It is now as commonplace to find a person on a social networking site as it once was to find them in the telephone book. In just the past few years, there has been an explosive and exponential growth of many networks.

Fraser and Dutta (2008, p. 4) point out that:

> "...the appeal of social networking sites cuts across national boundaries, aggregating networks representing every conceivable community. There are sites for business people: LinkedIn has 20 million members, Plaxo has 15 million and Xing has 4 million. BlackPlanet, a site for African-Americans, counts some 16 million members. There are also sites for doctors (Sermo), green activists (Care2), movie buffs (Flixster), photo-sharing (Flickr) and family reunion sites (Ancestry)."

As with many innovations, people were hesitant to accept the legitimate usage of social networking sites. Social networking sites can provide tools and opportunities that society has never had before. It has often been said that when a computer network connects people as well as machines, it becomes a social network (Garton, Haythornthwaite and Wellman, 1997; Newman, 2003; Wellman et al., 1996 as cited in Olsen, 2008).

At the time of publication of Nardi et al.'s (2002) article on professional networking, online professional networking sites such as LinkedIn were few and far between (Olsen, 2008). Since then there has been a rapid growth of such services and the number of social networking services that focus on professional networking online has become extensive (Boyd and Ellison, 2007 as cited in Olsen, 2008). Examples of popular social networking services that support professional networking include LinkedIn, CareerBuilder, Ecademy, Xing, Plaxo Pulse and Ryze (Olsen, 2008). As such, the Internet does not necessarily diminish the number of chains, but makes the chains more visible, which makes it easier to choose the 'right' paths (Olsen, 2008). To narrow the focus of this research, LinkedIn was chosen as the social networking service to be analysed as LinkedIn has seen an increased growth in terms of membership and usage in the past five years, provides a global foundation tool and has been ranked as one of the highest professional social networking services for businesses.

2.12.1 Definition of a social networking service

Business people conduct business differently with individual strategies and tactics. One method of business interaction is through a social networking service. A social network service focuses on building online content and communities of people who share common interests, or who are interested in exploring the interests of others. Advancements in technology have allowed most social network services to be web-based membership communities, thus allowing real time global interaction avoiding the confines of a brick and mortar meeting structure. Through social networking services, the Internet makes it easier to map out one's connections and discover how many chains separate individuals (Olsen, 2008). People might only be a few connections away from each other without even realizing it, and the social network services allow them to discover how and to whom they are connected (Adamic and Adar, 2005 as cited in Olsen 2008).

LinkedIn is a business-oriented social networking site mainly used by members for professional interaction rather than the social aspects of social networking service. LinkedIn's main purpose is "to provide business opportunities for professionals from all over the world through organizing and expanding one's professional network" (Olsen, 2008, p. 9).

The purpose of the LinkedIn site is to allow registered members to create and maintain a list of contact details of people they know and trust. The most important aspect of the service is the creation of one's own profile. The profile page can be considered the hub of a member's page, much like an online resume that highlights pervious work experience, educational qualifications, professional membership and references. Once this membership page is created, a member begins to create relationships with other LinkedIn members. Relationships between members are called connections. Members can invite anyone within the LinkedIn community to become a connection and can also invite non-LinkedIn members to join the community and connect. As LinkedIn is a closed invite connection (gate-access approach) system where contact between members requires either a pre-existing relationship or an invitation to connection with the need for acceptance of the invitation, trust is a very important aspect of the service. LinkedIn participates in the EU's International Safe Harbour Privacy Principles (LinkedIn, 2009).

In summation, a social network service focuses on building online content and communities of people who share common interests, or who are interested in exploring other interests. There are a number of social networking services currently available worldwide; however, for the purposes of this research, LinkedIn was chosen as the service to be researched.

LinkedIn is a business-oriented social networking site mainly used by members for professional interaction rather than the social aspects of social networking service.

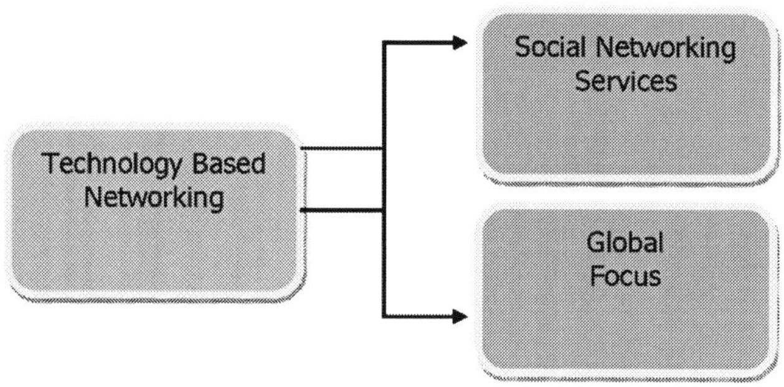

Figure 2.5: Technology Based Networking as fourth foundation of conceptual model

2.12.2 Use of LinkedIn as social networking tool

LinkedIn is a world-wide social networking service based in Silicon Valley that was officially launched on May 5, 2003. At the end of the first month in operation, the networking service had a total of 4,500 members in the network, and by the end of 2003 the number of members grew to

81,000 (with half of the membership from outside the USA), 14 total employees and $4.7M of investment (LinkedIn, 2009).

As of May 2009, LinkedIn had more than 40 million registered users, covering 170 industries. The community is available in English, Spanish, French and German and boasts membership from all Fortune 500 companies. (LinkedIn,2009).

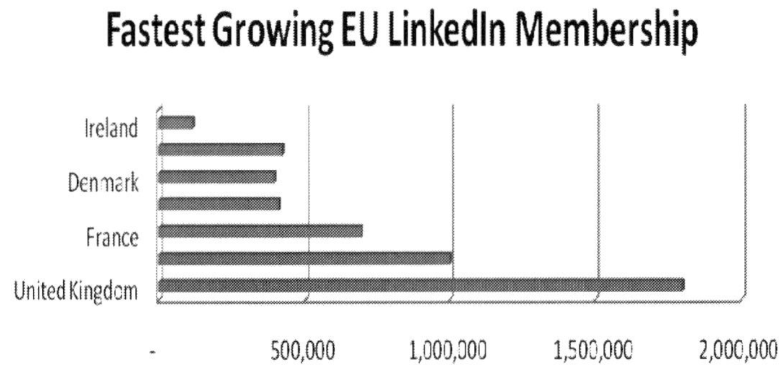

	United Kingdom	Netherlands	France	Belgium	Denmark	Germany	Ireland
Members	1,800,000	1,000,000	696,000	411,000	396,000	423,000	118,000

Figure 2.6: European LinkedIn membership as of March 2009 (LinkedIn, 2009)

From March 2007 through March 2008, LinkedIn had a growth of 319%, making it the fastest growing social networking service available (Bergfeld, 2008). LinkedIn users choose between free and premium accounts. The latter gives access to better tools for searching and communicating, making it easier to get in touch with new people (Olsen, 2008).

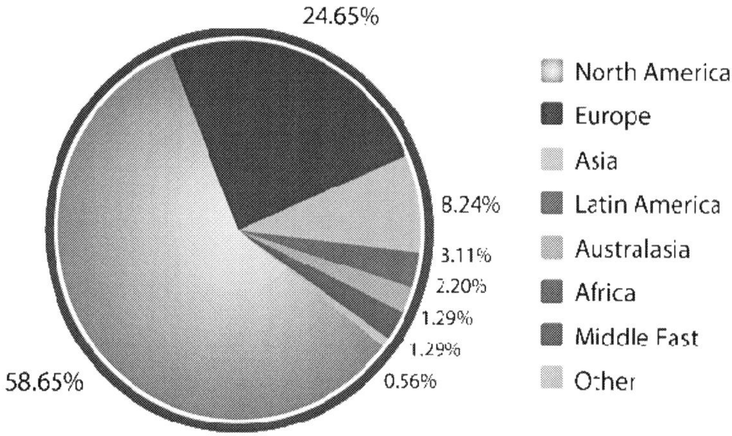

Figure 2.7: Global LinkedIn membership (LinkedIn, 2009)

The main purpose of LinkedIn is to provide business opportunities for professionals from all over the world through organizing, maintaining and expanding one's professional network (Olsen, 2008). As stated on the LinkedIn website:

> "LinkedIn is an interconnected network of experienced professionals from around the world, representing 170 industries and 200 countries. You can find, be introduced to, and collaborate with qualified professionals that you need to work with to accomplish your goals." (LinkedIn, 2009)

As highlighted on the LinkedIn website (LinkedIn, 2009), through the network a member can:

- Manage the information that is publicly available about a member;
- Find and be introduced to potential clients, service providers and subject experts;
- Create and collaborate on projects, gather data, share files and solve problems;
- Gain new insights from likeminded professionals in private discussion groups.

LinkedIn consists of a number of different features designed for presenting profiles, expanding networks and interaction between members. Many of these features are under constant development and new features emerge regularly (LinkedIn, 2009). Although some use LinkedIn as a pure sales tool, LinkedIn is more of a networking platform to start and maintain relationships. The consequence of building relationships might be a sale, but also a new job, finding a new employee, supplier, partner or expertise (Vermeiren, 2008).

The fact that LinkedIn has over 40 million members does not necessarily mean that all of them are active users (Olsen, 2008). The amount of time spent on LinkedIn is also likely to vary among members, and may change during one's membership (Olsen, 2008). Those members who use the network actively will, however, have access to a valuable networking tool when it comes to both nurturing and keeping track of existing connections, as well as getting in touch with other professionals (Olsen, 2008).

Boyd and Ellison (2007) emphasize that social networking services, such as LinkedIn, may provide a bridge between online and offline social relationships, and that they are particularly useful in relations to the maintenance of weak ties.

2.12.3 Entrepreneurial user types of LinkedIn

Business people use online social networking services like LinkedIn very differently (Anderson, 2008). Erwin Van Lun, futurist and trend analyst, described LinkedIn as an essential part of the new economy:

> "LinkedIn is not just a handy website or a tool to leverage your business, communicate with other people or find contacts. No, LinkedIn shows the foundation of an open, networked system that arises when we have cleaned up the capitalistic, closed system. In such a world new companies help people as a virtual coach in several domains. LinkedIn specializes in the "work" domain. This evolution in the new economy started with contacts, jobs and events. Then education, job orientation or mediation. When you project this to LinkedIn, you notice LinkedIn has just started. LinkedIn will evolve to a reliable companion in the whole work niche. Worldwide. LinkedIn is just at the beginning." (Vermeiren, 2008, p. 28)

Other type classifications determine first if the LinkedIn user is active or passive. Each use is then broken into two additional classifications – Active/Power Networker or Active/Productive and Passive/Unproductive Networker or Passive/Dormant Networker.

The following table highlights the traits of each of the four classifications (Olsen, 2008).

Active	Power networker	This type of networker is extremely active and interested in having as many connections as possible. The power networker will enthusiastically send out invitations, search for people and go through friends' connections in order to expand their own professional network. The power networker will generally spend much time on LinkedIn.
Active	Productive networker	The productive networker will actively send out invitations and search for connections, but not with the same enthusiasm as the power networker. The productive networker enjoys expanding their professional network and will spend the necessary time on LinkedIn in order to do so.
Passive	Unproductive networker	The unproductive networker does not spend much time on sending out invitations or search for new connections. The networker may log onto LinkedIn in order to accept connections, change their profile or get updates on existing connections, but this type of networker does not bother to do much about their membership.
Passive	Dormant networker	Dormant networkers are people who have registered as members on LinkedIn but have not yet started to use it. They hardly ever log onto LinkedIn and do not spend any time inviting or searching for connections.

Figure 2.8: Active versus Passive LinkedIn member

Olsen (2008) suggests that there also exist four types of networking strategies on LinkedIn:

Open/Unrestricted
Networkers that accept anyone as a connection. The networker is more concerned about being able to reach as many people as possible rather than knowing the people they are connected to.

Open/Regulated
Networkers that accept anyone as long as they see it as beneficial in relation to their own career. The networker screens on the basis of who they think could become useful in the future, or could represent interesting business opportunities. This type of networker does not need to know the people they are connected to, but there must be some common interest.

Closed/Regulated
Networkers that will only accept connections that they have had some previous contact with or that are respected in their industry. The networker does not need to have met a person in order to connect to them, but the connections need to be respected individuals in the same industry or someone he/she has communicated with previously.

Closed/Restricted
Networkers that only accept connections they trust or know. The networker is more concerned about knowing the people they are connect to rather than the overall size of the professional network. The connections can be people the networker has met briefly or only exchanged a few words with.

2.13 Conceptual framework

The conceptual framework identifies the areas of Irish entrepreneurship which were explored for the purpose of this research and is grounded in the theory on entrepreneurship, social capital and business networking which was reviewed throughout this chapter. The conceptual framework will assist the investigation of the importance of social capital, business networking and technology to the success of selected Irish entrepreneurs. The literature review explores the definitions of entrepreneurship, social capital and the development, growth and maintenance of a business network. The literature review also highlights that entrepreneurs are generally described as innovative, creative individuals who are determined, have a self-belief and are calculated risk takers (O'Gorman, 1997). The area of social capital has been widely examined, yet the topic of how an Irish entrepreneur uses technology to form, develop and maintain a business network is relatively unexplored due to its recent existence.

Figure 2.9 illustrates the starting point of the research concept, from the two-way relationship between business networking and social capital to the effects and perceived benefits of social networking, through the final relationship between business networking and effective use of technology to form, develop and maintain beneficial relationships.

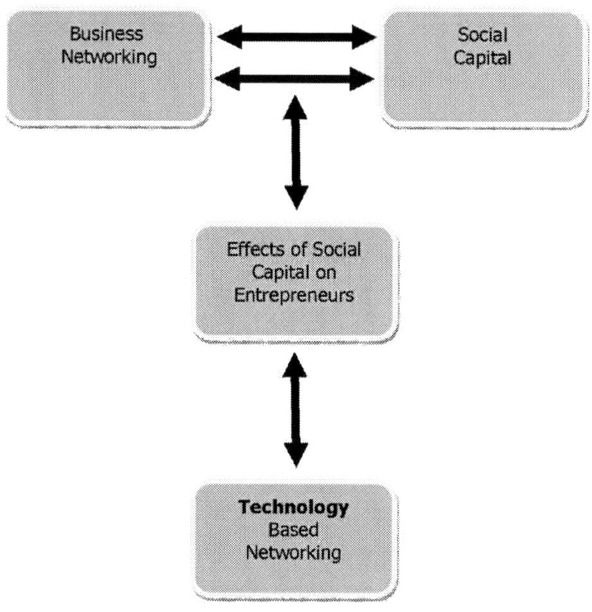

Figure 2.9: Conceptual Model

In summary, the conceptual framework is based upon the inter-relationship between business networking and social capital along with the effects of social capital on entrepreneurs and the increasing use of technology which provides a solid foundation upon which the research is presented. The relationship between social capital and technology based networking is represented as a dotted relationship, as the perception is that the Irish entrepreneur understands the value of social capital but prefers to network in-person and not by using technology. However, it is also perceived that this relationship is changing as there in an increasing need to network on a global basis, thus there is an increase in the use of technology to manage the overall network.

There is a business case for social capital with evidence that social capital increases business performance. Entrepreneurs with rich social capital enjoy access to venture capital and financing, improved organizational learning, the power of word-of-mouth marketing, the ability to create strategic alliances and resources to defend against hostile takeovers (Baker, 2000).

2.14 Conclusion

The literature review suggests that as entrepreneurs seek opportunities, it is essential to connect with a number of different stakeholders, and that by engaging with these different stakeholders entrepreneurs can gain valuable information that would otherwise be unavailable (Dana, 2001). With regards to Irish networking, the literature suggests that networking has gained popularity in Ireland over the past few years and that as both globalization and networking have begun to play an increasingly important role across Ireland, additional research is needed to understand the exact nature of the benefits of Irish networking. The literature identifies that benefits of networking can include but are not limited to the sharing of information, ideas, leads, business opportunities, financial capital, power, emotional support, goodwill, trust and cooperation (Baker, 2000). This research endeavours to establish what the perceived benefits of a business network to be for the Irish entrepreneur and how technology is used to form, develop and maintain a network. Building networks enables members of the network to contribute to others.

CHAPTER THREE

RESEARCH METHODOLOGY

3.1 Introduction

In this chapter, the use of qualitative methods will be introduced and the reason why qualitative research was used for this research will be clarified. Research as part of an academic process is conducted to investigate research questions that arise from existing literature on a topic of interest (Bryman and Bell, 2007). The design of the open-ended interview methodology is outlined including the elements of the interview. When deciding on which primary research method to use, it is first necessary to review all potential research methods (Creswell, 1994). Researchers remain divided and have debated greatly about which methodologies to use when conducting research (Amaratunga, 2002). Bryman and Bell (2007) suggest that there are four traditions of qualitative research: naturalism, ethnomethodology, emotionalism and postmodernism. The fact that four unique and contrasting traditions exist suggests to the difficulty of creating a definitive account of what qualitative research is, and what it is not (Bryman and Bell, 2007).

3.2 Qualitative research as the chosen methodology

A qualitative methodology was chosen for conducting this research. The social sciences have a long tradition of qualitative research (Ragin et al., 2003).

Many social science researchers such as Ragin and Dudwick acknowledge the importance of using a range of different methods to assess a given phenomenon. In practice, however, the distinctive skill sets associated with each approach, the complexity of the investigation and the limited time and resources, mean that only one approach tends to be adopted as was appropriate for this research (Dudwick et al., 2006). A minimalist definition of qualitative research is that qualitative research involves an in-depth study of a relatively small number of cases that seeks detailed knowledge of specific cases, often with the goal of finding out how things happen with a primary goal to make the facts understandable (Ragin, 2003). The Nvivo website (2009) suggests:

> "Qualitative research seeks out the 'why', not the 'how' of its topic through the analysis of unstructured information – things like interview transcripts and recordings, emails, notes, feedback forms, photos and videos. It doesn't just rely on statistics or numbers, which are the domain of quantitative researchers."

Details and additional information can be viewed at <www.nvivo.com>.

For these reasons, a qualitative research approach and methodology was deemed appropriate for this research as it allowed the researcher to gain a deeper understanding and insight into the Irish entrepreneur and their use of technology. When studying an ever changing online phenomenon like LinkedIn, the qualitative approach provides a number of advantages when trying to understand variables such as how, when and why the informant uses LinkedIn. With regards to data collection, the qualitative approach method's flexible and unstructured features make it possible to interpret the data in its own context, as well as providing a more in-depth description and understanding of the question at hand (Silverman, 2006).

Volery (2004) recommends qualitative methods for researching entrepreneurs as this type of research methodology allows the researcher to comprehensively observe individuals engaging in entrepreneurial activity within their natural environment. As entrepreneurship is one of the most recent concepts in the management sciences (Bygrave, 1989; Churchill and Lewis, 1986), it therefore has been recommended that research into this area should be based on empirical observations with grounded research (Bygrave, 1989). Other researchers supported similar ideas, as Low and MacMillian (1988) suggested that entrepreneurial research should continue to approach research by explaining rather than recording the entrepreneurial phenomenon.

The main steps in qualitative research as defined by Bryman and Bell (2007) are listed below:

1. General research questions
2. Selection of relevant sites and subjects
3. Collection of relevant data
4. Interpretation of data
5. Conceptual and theoretical work
    a. Tighter specification of the research question(s)
    b. Collection of further data
6. Writing up findings/conclusions

Much like improvements and innovations in technology can cause a dramatic change in how the improvements and innovations are used, it was important for this research to be able to measure how events and patterns would affect change over time. Bryman and Bell (2007) indicate that qualitative research tends to view social life in terms of a process, thereby illustrating why qualitative research is the appropriate choice for this research as the research aims to explore the ever changing technological social aspects of social capital and social networking.

3.3 Naturalism

The naturalistic approach is the chosen methodology for this research as it is more flexible and adaptable than positivism which concentrates on quantitative research methods and is inherently 'scientific' (Gill and Johnson, 1991; Hynes, 2002). Naturalism seeks to understand social reality in its own terms; as it really is and by so doing, provides a rich description of people and interaction in their natural settings.

Naturalism is used by a qualitative researcher who

> "Attempts to describe and interpret some human phenomenon, often in the words of selected individuals (the informants). These researchers try to be clear about their biases, presuppositions and interpretations so that others (the stakeholders) can decide what they think about it all." (Heath, 1997, p. 2)

The naturalistic approach also recognizes that it is through the research that an intimate relationship can be created between the researcher and the subject matter; and therefore includes flexible research methods such as in-depth interviews, observation, documentation and archival methods (Gill and Johnson, 1991). The fundamental component of naturalism is that it stresses the subjective part of each individual by recognizing that 'objective knowledge' is unattainable (Hynes, 2002).

As this research involves a profound understanding of why an Irish entrepreneur would use technology such as LinkedIn to complete networking activities, the naturalistic approach is the most appropriate methodology due to its flexibility and adaptability (Gill and Johnson, 1991). This is further supported by O'Donnell and Cummins (1999) who cited that a qualitative methodology is the most appropriate research approach when researching networking activities as it allowed the activity to be examined in its social context and enabled the researcher to better connect with the subjects.

3.4 The semi-structured interview research method

The semi-structured interview method was chosen for conducting the qualitative research for this study. As this research focused on the specific reasoning on how the Irish entrepreneur used LinkedIn for their business, it was determined that a semi-structured interview research method was the most advantageous for data collection. The interview method of data collection is one of the many options with regards to a research interview. Research analysis has shown that a semi-structured interview method is most commonly used for qualitative survey research (Bryman and Bell, 2007). The goal of a semi-structured interview is for the interviewing of entrepreneurs to be as standardized as possible so that the difference between each interview can be minimised (Bryman and Bell, 2007) while also allowing the researcher a chance to explore each answer more thoroughly if needed. The aim of the research was to elicit from the entrepreneur their attitudes, norms, beliefs and values with regard to their use of LinkedIn.

A semi-structured interview is a conversation(s) between the researcher and the entrepreneur based on a pre-established interview guide. After an introduction which includes an explanation of the interview, including confidentiality, the main topic is given, the questions are prepared in a broad and open manner, and subsequent questions are asked dependent on the conversation (Silverman, 2006). While the interview guide provides the semi-structure of the interview including the pertinent questions to ask, the semi-structure allows the researcher to follow-up on interesting responses, allows new topics to arise within the process and provides the researcher the opportunity to be not only an active listener, but also an active participant in the process.

Silverman (2006, p. 292) suggests:

> "...in order to achieve rich data, the keynote is active listening in which the interviewer allows the interviewee the freedom to talk and ascribe meanings while bearing in mind the broader aims of the project."

It is the standardisation of both the asking of the questions and the proper recording of the answers that provides the true variations of individual responses and not due to the interview context (Bryman and Bell, 2007).

3.4.1 Vignette questions

As part of the in-depth interview method, a number of vignette questions were used. Vignette questioning is a form of asking mainly closed questions that have been used in connection with the examination of the respondent's normative standards (Bryman and Bell, 2007). The technique presents respondents with one or more scenarios and then asks them how they (the respondent) would respond when confronted with the circumstances of that scenario (Bryman and Bell, 2007). The main advantage of the vignette is that it anchors the choice in a situation and as such decreases the possibility of an unreflective reply (Bryman and Bell, 2007). In addition, vignette can also decrease the sensitivity of questions and thus allow distance between the questioning and the respondent (Bryman and Bell, 2007).

3.4.2 The interview guide

The interview guide was created prior to the interview sessions and included instructions for the researcher, the complete list of interview questions and answers to the most frequently asked questions regarding the interview. The complete interview guide is shown in Appendix 1.

Particular attention was given in the creation of the interview guide to ensure that clear instructions were given with regards to the semi-structured interview including the progress through the interview session. The interview guide provided the researcher with the ability to accurately gauge the session time management. Importance was also given to the question order as set forth prior to the interview session in the interview guide. This was done to ensure that all questions were asked and to avoid variation of the entrepreneur's answers based on different question order.

The interviews were scheduled to take 45 minutes, with a plus/minus variance given based upon the interaction between the researcher and the entrepreneur. Prior to the start of all interviews, the interview guide, flow of the questions and recording capabilities were tested and approved by the research supervisor.

There was a combination of both open-ended and close-ended questions used in the interview guide. There were a total of 29 questions in the interview. The majority of the questions were closed questions (23). These questions enhanced the interview guide by allowing for comparability of the answers, making it easier to show the relationship between variables and to make comparisons between respondents (Bryman and Bell, 2007). The remaining questions were open ended (6 main topic areas with 46 sub-topic questions). This decision was based on the advantages of the open-ended question method. It was determined that since the entrepreneurs could answer the specific question in their own terms (not forced to answer the questions in a certain way as in closed- ended questions) and since the questions would foster an atmosphere that allowed for unusual responses that could then be further discussed, it was important to allow for such responses (Bryman and Bell, 2007).

3.4.3 The data collection procedure

This research is based on interviews with ten self-identified Irish entrepreneurs that have a LinkedIn account. There were six males and four females interviewed. Participants were the researchers' own Irish connections and the connections of others. The only limiting consideration was that each participant needed to have an active LinkedIn account. Frequency of LinkedIn use was not used to determine participation in the research. Additional participants were available for the research; however, it was determined by the researcher that additional interviews would not elicit further insight into that which was being observed.

As the overall usage of LinkedIn was over 40 million at the time of this research, it was necessary to select a much smaller subset to analyse from the overall LinkedIn population that was manageable yet large enough to answer the fundamental questions of the research.

Previous research has identified that there are two main categories of sampling: probability sampling and non-probability sampling (Remenyi et al., 2005). Due to the large potential sample size, a non-probability sampling was chosen. In addition, a combination of purposive sampling and snowball sampling was determined to be the best method of sampling for this research.

Figure 3.1: Location of Entrepreneurial Respondents in Ireland

3.4.4 Sampling

Purposive sampling is a sample method created from a purpose, usually based on predefined qualities that the researcher is seeking (Remenyi, 2005). This was an important characteristic of sampling for this research as the entrepreneurs needed to have an active LinkedIn account rather than simply being registered as members of the networking service. While other research in this area also considered the number of connections an entrepreneur had as a defining factor for participation in the research, it was determined that since LinkedIn was a relatively new service in Ireland, no limiting factor other than an active membership would be used.

Snowball sampling was also used to find potential respondents for this research. Snowball sampling allows for existing respondents to recommend other potential respondents that could fulfill the necessary criteria. However, one area of concern with this approach was that snowball sampling can often create a situation where it is more likely that certain subgroups will be over-represented. Entrepreneurs that are connected to others often tend to have similar interests and it is therefore likely a recommend of potential respondents that are similar to themselves. For this reason, special attention was introduced to ensure that a proper demographic mixture was used for this research sampling.

After identifying a number of entrepreneurs by the use of purposive sampling, the entrepreneurs were contacted and asked to participate in the research study. The entrepreneurs were also asked for additional Irish LinkedIn users that might be interested in participation. From a sample of over 25 entrepreneurs, 10 were interviewed. After the 10th interview, the responses started to repeat, thus the point of saturation had been reached. The number of respondents was not set prior to the start of the interviews. This was because it is often difficult to estimate when the value of each interview decreases (Jacobson, 2005).

In quantitative research, data collection often occurs well in advance of data analysis. Ragin et al. (2003, p. 12) suggests:

> "If data analysis indicates that additional data collection is needed, it usually occurs in a subsequent study. Researchers analyse data as they collect them and often decide what data to collect next based on what they have learned. Thus, in qualitative research it is often a challenge to specify a structured data collection and analysis plan in advance".

All interviews were recorded and transcribed. Three interviews (Interview 2, Interview 7 and Interview 8) were conducted in person as the interviews were located near the researcher. The other seven interviews were conducted via Skype. To ensure that there was no bias in the face-to-face or Skype interview methods, the same script of the interview questions was used. Recordings were done to ensure comprehensive collection of all data and transcribed afterwards to avoid a loss of information (Anda and Hove, 2005). Quotes used in this research which were taken from interviews and demonstrate the various views which were expressed by the responding entrepreneurs. The average number of LinkedIn connections at the time of their respective interviews was 117. The maximum number of connections was 230 with the fewest being 11.

3.4.5 Interviews

The interviews were conducted over a one-month period and the duration of the interviews varied from thirty minutes to one hour and fifteen minutes. The researcher conducted each interview based on the criteria previously set forth in the interview guide in section 3.4.2. The questions investigated the following general areas:

- Demographic information
- Reasons for social networking
- Perceived benefits of LinkedIn
- Expectations and limitations of LinkedIn
- How does LinkedIn assist with regard to establishing, maintaining and developing relations?

All responding entrepreneurs were asked about the areas of exploration as outlined above. None of the subjects refused to answer any of the questions.

3.5 Criteria for analysis

As qualitative data collected during interviews can produce vast amounts of information, a defined strategy is needed to organize the data in a systematic and relevant manner (Yin, 2003). Marshall and Rossman (1995, p. 111) define data analysis as

> "...the process of bringing order, structure and meaning to the mass of collected data. It is a messy, ambiguous, time-consuming, creative and fascinating process. It does not proceed in a linear fashion; it is not neat. Qualitative data analysis is a search for general statements about relationships among categories of data."

There are three activities which comprise data analysis: data reduction, data display and conclusion drawing/verification (Miles and Huberman, 1984). Data reduction is the process of selecting, simplifying, extracting and altering the basic research data (Miles and Huberman, 1984). Data display is the process of displaying the collected data in order to allow conclusions to be created. The conclusion drawing/verification process involves drawing meaning from data and constructing a logical sequence of evidence (Miles and Huberman, 1984). Data reduction can arise through the selection of a conceptual framework and is accomplished via summaries, coding, extrapolating themes, making clusters, making subsets and writing memos (Miles and Huberman, 1984). The design of a data display is a distinct analytical process, as well as a type of data reduction (Miles and Huberman, 1984). At the first stage of analysis the researcher establishes what the data denotes by attempting to identify consistent patterns, propositions and explanations (Miles and Huberman, 1984).

Questions for the interview were based on a similar research study by Olsen in 2008. In the research, a Likert scale was used. Likert scales are a common ratings format for surveys. Entrepreneurs rank quality from high to low or best to worst using five or seven levels (Allen and Seaman, 2007). For this research, a five-point scale was used.

Accordingly, a high score (5 or 4) indicated high satisfaction with the question and a low score (1 or 2) for a question indicated a low satisfaction with the question. One advantage of a closed set of questions is that the questions can be pre-coded, thus turning the process of analysis into a fairly simple task (Bryman and Bell, 2007).

3.6 Collecting evidence

Ten Irish entrepreneurs agreed to participate in the interview process and the information collected was gathered to build a spreadsheet. The subjects could be male or female, of any age and had to have an active LinkedIn account. Activity level on their LinkedIn account was not an interviewing limiting factor. As the interview was designed to be virtual and could be conducted over Skype, there was no geographical limitation other than being of Irish nationality. Potential subjects were not limited to a certain ethnic group and any entrepreneur who met the inclusion criteria could participate. The selection was not limited to one sector as this was deemed as being too restrictive and would limit the pool of potential responding entrepreneurs for the research. One in-depth interview per entrepreneur was the sole research method utilized. The interviews were conducted over a one-month period in the Spring of 2009.

3.7 Data Analysis

Yin (2003) defines data analysis the process of examining, categorising, charting or otherwise amalgamating the evidence in order to address the initial intentions of the study. Because qualitative data collection from interviews typically takes the form of large amounts of unstructured textual materials, the data is not always straightforward to analyse; thus clear-cut rules about how this data should be analysed have not been developed (Bryman and Bell, 2007). Qualitative research is about exploring issues, understanding phenomena and answering questions (Nvivo, 2009).

There is usually an overlap between data collection and analysis in qualitative research, which allows the research to be refocused and a suitable theoretical sampling to be conducted throughout the course of the research (Eisenhardt, 1989; Glaser and Strauss, 1967; Strauss and Corbin, 1998).

According to Eisenhardt (1989, p. 539) this flexibility is advantageous for researchers as it allows them to:

> "...take advantage of the uniqueness of a specific case and the emergence of new themes to improve resultant theory".

Qualitative research data analysis has indicated that there are two strategies of analysis: analytic induction and grounded theory (Bryman and Bell, 2007). For the purposes of this research, a grounded theory approach was taken. As defined by Bryman and Bell (2007, p. 585), grounded theory is

> "...theory that was derived from data systematically gathered and analysed through the research process where the data collection, analysis and eventual theory stand in close relationship to one another."

The coding of the data in grounded theory is one of the most central processes in grounded theory as it entails reviewing the transcriptions and giving labels to component parts that seem to be of potential theoretical significance and that also appear to be salient with that which is being studied (Bryman and Bell, 2007). This code serves as shorthand device to label, separate, compile and organize data (Charmaz, 1983). As Charmaz (2000) (cited in Bryman and Bell, 2007, p. 585) suggests,

> "we grounded theorists code our emerging data as we collect it."

In order to produce research of the highest quality, Yin (2003) presented four guidelines that the researcher should aim to achieve:

1. The findings should show that the analysis was based on all the relevant evidence.
2. All major rival interpretations in the analysis should be included in the research.
3. The most important aspect of the case study should be addressed.
4. The researcher should use previous expert knowledge to develop the analysis further.

Qualitative research software helps researchers classify, manage and make sense of unstructured information providing a sophisticated workspace that helps discover patterns, identify themes and develop conclusions (Nvivo, 2009). For the purpose of this research, it was determined that using common Microsoft Office programs such as Microsoft Word and Microsoft Excel would suffice due to time constraints and the relatively low number of responding entrepreneurs needed for research.

Reliability refers to the consistency of a measure of a concept (Bryman and Bell, 2007). When conducting a study based on human subjects, there are several issues that need to be addressed as human nature is known for its inconsistency as people are distracted, can misinterpret and sometimes lie (Olsen, 2008). This would suggest that it is nearly impossible to calculate reliability and that is can only be estimated (Olsen, 2008). In addition, the interpretation of the data might not be entirely reliable as the researcher may interpret situations in a different manner than the entrepreneur intended:

> "…even when people's activities are audio or video recorded and transcribed, the reliability of the interpretation of transcripts may be gravely weakened by a failure to note apparently trivial, but often crucial, pauses, overlaps or body movements." (Silverman, 2006, p. 46)

To provide the best possible analysis of the data, it was determined that the digital recording of all interviews and subsequent transcription would ensure the greatest reliability.

Validity refers to the issue of whether or not an indicator (or set of indicators) that is devised to gauge a concept really measures that concept (Bryman and Bell, 2007). As also defined by Bryman and Bell (2007), there are five prominent factors used to establish validity:

- Face validity – the measure apparently reflects the content of the concept in question,

- Concurrent validity – use of a criterion on which cases are known to differ,
- Predictive validity – the researcher uses a future criterion measure rather than a contemporary one,
- Construct validity – the researcher is encouraged to deduce hypotheses from a theory that is relevant to the concept,
- Convergent validity – the validity of a measurement should be gauged by comparing it to a measure of the same concept developed through other methods.

Validity can also be related to whether or not the research design is suitable for collecting data relevant to the research, and to which degree what has been measured match what was supposed to be measured (Remenyi et al., 2004; Silverman, 2006). Validity is often associated with the credibility and dependability of the qualitative research -- are the results believable (Olsen, 2008). It can be argued that only the respondents themselves know if the researcher's interpretations are correct (Olsen, 2008).

The research carried out was aimed at gaining an understanding of how an Irish entrepreneur uses technology to manage, maintain and develop their business network, and thus their social capital. A detailed literature review formulated very specific research objectives. The research objectives evolved through an on-going process interlinked with the amassing of data from the literature review and continually developing as the data from the interviews became apparent and the questions were refined (Robson, 1993).

3.8 Research objective one: the perceived benefits of networking

Research Objective One aims to ascertain the perceived benefits of networking. This was explored in the context of the literature review which identified entrepreneurship as a field of business that seeks to understand how opportunities to create something new (innovation) are discovered or created by individuals who then use various means to exploit or develop them, and in so doing can produce a wide range of outcomes (Baron and Shane, 2005). It is through such innovation that business networking becomes important since the economics of entrepreneurship is socially embedded (Cope et al., 2007).

In order to answer the first research question, the following areas on why an Irish entrepreneur uses LinkedIn were explored. The motivations for the type of networking by the Irish entrepreneur were examined first.

3.8.1 Career Opportunity / New Venture Creation / Expertise Requests / Staying Connected / Future Business Opportunity / Partnership / Personal Networking / Research / Sales Prospecting

- An Irish entrepreneur for whom [Career Opportunity / New Venture Creation / Expertise Requests / Staying Connected / Future Business Opportunity / Partnership / Personal Networking / Research / Sales Prospecting] within the network has strong significance as a motivation for being part of a business network will cite [Career Opportunity / New Venture Creation / Expertise Requests / Staying Connected / Future Business Opportunity / Partnership / Personal Networking / Research / Sales Prospecting] as the main reason for wanting to be part of said network.
- An Irish entrepreneur for whom [Career Opportunity / New Venture Creation / Expertise Requests / Staying Connected / Future Business Opportunity / Partnership / Personal Networking / Research / Sales Prospecting] within the network has moderate significance as a motivation for being part of a business network will not cite [Career Opportunity / New Venture Creation / Expertise Requests / Staying Connected / Future Business Opportunity / Partnership / Personal Networking / Research / Sales Prospecting] as the main reason for wanting to be part of said network, but may refer to it as being a contributing factor.
- An Irish entrepreneur for whom [Career Opportunity / New Venture Creation / Expertise Requests / Staying Connected / Future Business Opportunity / Partnership / Personal Networking / Research / Sales Prospecting] within the network has weak significance as a motivation for being part of a business network will not cite [Career Opportunity / New Venture Creation / Expertise Requests / Staying Connected / Future Business Opportunity / Partnership / Personal Networking / Research / Sales Prospecting] as the main reason for wanting to be part of said network.

3.9 Research objective two: The formation, maintenance and development of entrepreneurial networks

Research Objective Two explores how the Irish entrepreneur forms, maintains and develops his or her network. In order to answer this research question, the significance of online versus offline networking was investigated and the researcher aimed to establish who comprises the networks. Lynch et al. (2009) suggests that 'business networking' is not an end in itself but rather a means to enhancing business performance and efficiency.

The formation of the business network was explored in the context of the literature review which identified a three-phase approach that networkers need to achieve to create a successful professional network, which include building a network, maintaining the network and activating selected contacts (Nardi et al., 2002). The literature review also suggested that networkers need to continue to add new contacts to their network in order to access as many resources as possible, and to maintain their network through staying in touch with their contacts (Olsen, 2008).

The development of the network was analysed by an initial number of connections that was then compared to a three-month review of the number of connections, while considering the networker's reported propensity of LinkedIn usage. In addition, the measurement of whether an entrepreneur lived outside of Ireland for over six months was analysed to determine if such an action had an effect of the number of non-Irish connections on LinkedIn. The literature review also provided a framework for the types of LinkedIn user and the strategies with regards to how the network is developed. Olsen (2008) established Active vs. Passive networking and Open vs. Closed networking as the measurement for the types of networkers and the development of said network. This research continues with Olsen's model and has plotted the information from the Irish entrepreneur study under the same guidelines as per the literature review.

3.9.1 Active Networking

- An Irish entrepreneur for whom active networking has strong significance as a motivation for being part of a business network will cite 'proactively seeking out new connections' as the main reason for networking.
- An Irish entrepreneur for whom active networking has moderate significance as a motivation for being part of a business network will

not cite 'proactively seeking out new connections' as the main reason for networking, but may refer to it as being a contributing factor.

- An Irish entrepreneur for whom active networking has weak significance as a motivation for being part of a business network will not cite 'proactively seeking out new connections' as the main reason for wanting to be part of said network.

3.9.2 Passive Networking

- An Irish entrepreneur for whom passive networking has strong significance as a motivation for being part of a business network will cite 'slow and controlled network growth' as the main reason for networking.
- An Irish entrepreneur for whom passive networking has moderate significance as a motivation for being part of a business network will not cite 'slow and controlled network growth' as the main reason for networking, but may refer to it as being a contributing factor.
- An Irish entrepreneur for whom passive networking has weak significance as a motivation for being part of a business network will not cite 'slow and controlled network growth' as the main reason for networking.

3.9.3 Open Networking

- An Irish entrepreneur for whom open networking has strong significance as a motivation for being part of a business network will suggest 'connecting with everyone' as the goal for networking and will show a dramatic increase in the number of connections over a three-month period.
- An Irish entrepreneur for whom open networking has moderate significance as a motivation for being part of a business network will not cite 'connecting with everyone' as a goal for networking as the main reason for networking, but may refer to it as being a contributing factor and will show a moderate increase in the number of connections over a three- month period.
- An Irish entrepreneur for whom open networking has weak significance as a motivation for being part of a business network will not cite 'connecting with everyone' as the main reason for networking and will not show an increase in the number of connections over a three- month period.

3.9.4 Closed Networking

- An Irish entrepreneur for whom closed networking has strong significance as a motivation for being part of a business network will suggest 'the importance of knowing everyone in the network' as the goal for networking.
- An Irish entrepreneur for whom closed networking has moderate significance as a motivation for being part of a business network will not cite 'the importance of knowing everyone in the network' as the main reason for networking, but may refer to it as being a contributing factor.
- An Irish entrepreneur for whom closed networking has weak significance as a motivation for being part of a business network will not cite 'the importance of knowing everyone in the network' as the goal for networking.

3.10 Research objective three: the use of technology to manage social capital

Research Objective Three explores how the Irish entrepreneur uses technology to manage social capital. In order to answer this research question, the use of technology within social capital, the differences between online and offline management of social capital and the use of LinkedIn as the chosen online tool to manage social capital were investigated. The researcher aimed to establish the reasons for an entrepreneur to use technology to manage social networks and the perceived values of such usage were identified through literature review and individual interviews. The literature review established that a social network service, such as LinkedIn, focuses on building online content and communities of people who share common interests, or who are interested in exploring the interests others. The literature review specific to LinkedIn is to provide business opportunities for professionals from all over the world through organizing, maintaining and expanding one's professional network (Olsen, 2008).

3.10.1 Use of technology with social capital

- An Irish entrepreneur for whom technology is strongly significant to networking will use technology on multiple times per day.
- An Irish entrepreneur for whom technology is moderately significant to networking will use technology on a daily basis.

- An Irish entrepreneur for whom technology is not significant to networking will not use technology.

3.10.2 Importance of Online Networking

- An Irish entrepreneur for whom online networking has strong significance as the preferred method of networking will suggest the importance of online networking as the most effective method of networking.
- An Irish entrepreneur for whom online networking has moderate significance as the preferred method of networking will not suggest the importance of online networking as the most effective method of networking but may refer to it as being a contributing factor.
- An Irish entrepreneur for whom online networking has weak significance as the preferred method of networking will not cite the importance of online networking as the most effective method of networking.

3.10.3 Growth of Online Network

- An Irish entrepreneur for whom online networking has strong significance as the preferred method of networking will have a significant increase in the number of online connections within LinkedIn over a three- month period.
- An Irish entrepreneur for whom online networking has moderate significance as the preferred method of networking will have a moderate increase in the number of online connections within LinkedIn over a three- month period.
- An Irish entrepreneur for whom online networking has weak significance as the preferred method of networking will have a small increase in the number of online connections within LinkedIn over a three- month period.

3.11 Conclusion

In summary, this chapter has described the research approach and discussed the reasons for the methodology used while conducting the research project. The objectives of this research are threefold: first, to review the perceived benefits of networking; second, to access the formation, maintenance and development of entrepreneurial networks; and third, to analyse the use of technology to manage social capital. The method used for gathering the data for analysis for the project was a combination of semi-structured interviews and vignette questioning. The sampling method of finding respondents was purposive and snowball effect and the method of analysis for the research was cross analysis and assessment against existing theoretical propositions. The criteria for analysis were outlined and all variables were based on the literature review as presented in Chapter 2.

CHAPTER FOUR

PRIMARY RESEARCH FINDINGS

This chapter addresses the analysis based upon the research objectives as established in Chapter One. Chapter Two focused upon the literature review while Chapter Three illustrated the variables for each research objective. The themes and topics that have risen throughout the collection of data will be reviewed and elaborated. The findings will be analysed according to the literature review, the entrepreneur approach to social networking and how the entrepreneur makes use of social networking services, more specifically the use of LinkedIn.

4.1 Entrepreneur profile

The average age range of the entrepreneurs was 32-36 years old, with six male entrepreneurs and four female entrepreneurs. All entrepreneurs used the free version of LinkedIn, with an average of 3.7 employees within the entrepreneur's company. Different lengths of LinkedIn membership (in months) and different numbers of connections were included in the research. The average length of membership on LinkedIn was 18.2 months, with a minimum length of 6 months and a maximum length of 48 months.

Regarding the number of connections, there were an average number of 117 connections, with a minimum of 11 connections and a maximum of 230 connections. Concerning usage of LinkedIn, 3 entrepreneurs reported using LinkedIn more than once per day (Entrepreneurs 1, 5 and 10), 3 entrepreneurs reported daily use of LinkedIn (Entrepreneurs 4, 6 and 9) and 4 entrepreneurs reported weekly use of LinkedIn (Entrepreneurs 2, 3, 7 and 8).

Respondent	Age	Gender	Number of Employees	Type	Number of Connections	Member for (in months)	Site usage
1	30-34	M	5	Free	230	18	Many times per day
2	35-39	F	3	Free	76	48	Weekly
3	25-29	M	1	Free	92	12	Weekly
4	30-34	M	6	Free	180	30	Daily
5	35-39	M	1	Free	189	24	Many times per day
6	30-34	F	10	Free	77	6	Daily
7	35-39	F	3	Free	39	8	Weekly
8	40-44	F	2	Free	11	6	Weekly
9	30-34	M	3	Free	114	10	Daily
10	25-29	M	3	Free	162	36	Many times per day

Table 4.1: Summary of entrepreneur demographics

4.2 Analysis of Objective One: The perceived benefits of networking

Research Objective One explored the entrepreneur's perceived benefits of networking with regards to Irish entrepreneurship. The data illustrated that the top three perceived benefits of social networking were partnership opportunity, staying connected and future business opportunity. The lowest three ranked perceived benefits were career opportunities, sales prospecting and expertise requests.

Career Opportunity	3.7
Sales Prospecting	2.6
Expertise Requests	2.4
New Ventures	2.3
Personal Networking	2.2
Research	1.9
Partnership Opportunity	1.8
Stay Connected	1.6
Future Business Opportunity	1.5

Table 4.2: Ranking of perceived benefits

Many entrepreneurs reported that a well-established network is more than a contact list that is used to call others when help is needed. Entrepreneur 2 described how the more they used LinkedIn, the more it was becoming part of how they connected with the network.

It was also suggested that an online business network that shares information between weak connections has limitations of trust. Entrepreneur 2 saw the need for privacy of information as part of that trust and expressed concerns with a website where anyone could see a snapshot of details about the company. For them, sharing information was on a need-to- know basis.

Entrepreneur 7 suggests:

> "While I see the value of LinkedIn with my international connections, I don't think the Irish culture sees the value or has made the transition from understanding the ease of use in using the service. The first place I post an update is on my own corporate website, and that takes me sending an email to the website developer to make the programming change. If I understand correctly, LinkedIn can basically serve the same function and it is something I can do without the need for IT involvement. I just need to make that system work and let my connections know I am going to do it."

One of the challenges that entrepreneurs reported was at what stage of adoption the rest of the network was with regards to the use of LinkedIn. Entrepreneur 1 suggested that they were a more advanced user of LinkedIn when compared to their Irish peers, but behind the curve when compared to their American counterparts. Entrepreneur 1 theorized that Americans are early adaptors of LinkedIn technology compared to Irish users. However, Entrepreneur 1 also suggested that as their contacts became more comfortable with LinkedIn, the networking service became a more powerful business tool.

The following perceived benefits of networking were analysed:

Career Opportunity
New Venture Creation
Expertise Requests
Staying Connected
Future Business Opportunity
Partnership
Personal Networking
Research
Sales Prospecting

4.2.1 Career Opportunity

The first issue which was explored was the perceived importance of using the network for Career Opportunity. The analysis of the interview data suggests that Career Opportunity was the lowest ranked perceived benefit from a business network. The overall score was 3.7 out of 5.0 with one of the ten entrepreneurs (Entrepreneur 5) scoring Career Opportunity as Strongly Agree or Agree, three (Entrepreneurs 3, 4 and 10) scoring as neutral and six entrepreneurs (Entrepreneurs 1, 2, 6, 7, 8 and 9) scoring as Strongly Disagree.

Career Opportunity	3.7				
	Strongly Agree	Agree	Neutral	Disagree	Strongly Disagree
Entrepreneur 1					x
Entrepreneur 2					x
Entrepreneur 3			x		
Entrepreneur 4			x		
Entrepreneur 5	x				
Entrepreneur 6				x	
Entrepreneur 7				x	
Entrepreneur 8					x
Entrepreneur 9				x	
Entrepreneur 10			x		

Table 4.3: Career Opportunity

Entrepreneur 4 stated:

> "I'd say it's probably 3 or 4 years since I updated my CV, so what I do now is give people my personalized LinkedIn address because it has more information -- it's more regularly updated. It has my recommendations from other people and people can dig in and see whatever they want about my work experience and my history."

Entrepreneur 3 stated that LinkedIn gave the perception of an extra level of credibility, where the network can review the connection's expertise, their background and their past work experience, all making it easier to foster new career opportunities.

In summary, the perceived benefit of networking related to career opportunity with regard to this research would suggest that the respondents indicated a low perception to advances in career opportunity with networking. Career opportunity was ranked as the lowest of the nine perceived benefits as reported by the interviewed entrepreneurs. The vast majority of people do not find jobs through advertisements, head-hunters, electronic bulletin boards or other 'formal' methods. More people find career opportunities through personal connections than by any other means (Baker, 2000). The responses from the entrepreneurs do not support this statement.

4.2.2 New Ventures

The next issue which was explored was the perceived importance of using the network for New Ventures. The overall score for New Ventures was 2.3 out of 5.0, with four of the ten entrepreneurs (Entrepreneurs 3, 4, 5 and 10) scoring this perceived benefit as Strongly Agree, two (Entrepreneurs 2 and 6) as Agree, one (Entrepreneur 9) as Neutral, three (Entrepreneurs 1, 7 and 8) as Disagree. Table 4.4 illustrates the responses of the entrepreneurs, indicating the perceived value of New Ventures as important to networking.

New Ventures	2.3				
	Strongly Agree	Agree	Neutral	Disagree	Strongly Disagree
Entrepreneur 1				x	
Entrepreneur 2		x			
Entrepreneur 3	x				
Entrepreneur 4	x				
Entrepreneur 5	x				
Entrepreneur 6		x			
Entrepreneur 7				x	
Entrepreneur 8				x	
Entrepreneur 9			x		
Entrepreneur 10	x				

Table 4.4: New Ventures

Entrepreneur 5 reported the importance of using their network with a goal of purely seeking new opportunities:

> "While media and public relations are important for business marketing and growth, I see the importance of assessing individuals you might meet and see who they know you might know as well. Whether it is an employee of a company or a friend of a friend, I try to leverage that opportunity."

Other entrepreneurs reported different perceived value in using LinkedIn. For example, Entrepreneur 3 saw LinkedIn as one of the many tools available to grow business, as their LinkedIn network fills the space of a various business contact tool into one complete system to find new business opportunities. Entrepreneur 3 noted that their network grows every day, presenting an opportunity to connect with potential customers and business partners.

In summary, the perceived benefit of networking related to new ventures with regard to this research would suggest that the respondents indicated a moderate perception to advances in new venture activity with networking. New ventures was ranked as the sixth of the nine perceived benefits as reported by the interviewed entrepreneurs. The entrepreneurs tended to be conscious of professional networking and the potential new ventures that might be enabled by such activity. The US Small Business Administration sponsored a series of surveys to examine how small businesses and entrepreneurs get venture capital financing. The findings report that seventy-five percent of start-ups and new businesses find and secure financing through the social network of capital seekers and investors. This 'informal capital market' is estimated to be so large that the amount of capital it provides is much greater than the financing supplied via the professional venture capital market (Baker, 2000), thus supporting the importance of networking and new ventures.

4.2.3 Expertise Requests

The next issue that was explored was the perceived importance of using the network for Expertise Requests. The overall score for Expertise Requests was 2.4 out of 5.0 with one of the ten entrepreneurs (Entrepreneur 2) scoring this perceived benefit as Strongly Agree, five (Entrepreneurs 3, 4, 7, 8 and 9) as Agree, three (Entrepreneurs 5, 6 and 10) as Neutral and one (Entrepreneur 1) as Disagree. Table 4.5 illustrates:

Expertise Requests	2.4				
	Strongly Agree	Agree	Neutral	Disagree	Strongly Disagree
Entrepreneur 1				x	
Entrepreneur 2	x				
Entrepreneur 3		x			
Entrepreneur 4		x			
Entrepreneur 5			x		
Entrepreneur 6			x		
Entrepreneur 7		x			
Entrepreneur 8		x			
Entrepreneur 9		x			
Entrepreneur 10			x		

Table 4.5: Expertise Requests

Entrepreneur 7 commented on how they used their LinkedIn network to gain information about a business trip to St. Petersburg, Russia, including information on the Russian entrepreneurial culture, St. Petersburg city information (places to see, restaurants of choice and areas to avoid) and to schedule a business meeting that led to a successful business partnership.

Entrepreneur 5 viewed their own LinkedIn profile as a source of expertise for others in the network:

> "I had never thought of my business network as more than a list of connections until I began using LinkedIn. I see it as more than an online CV, because it adds links to their references and to me that adds credibility to you as an individual. I can contact the reference with a click of a button. It can be much more powerful than even I suggest."

Entrepreneur 4 has vast experience within the information technology community and sees value in finding others that have previous experience with a person or service specific to the iPhone market. They use LinkedIn groups to find qualified experts to answer questions about the technology in real time and to provide assistance to others that are in need of answers themselves.

In summary, the perceived benefit of networking to expertise requests with regard to this research would suggest that the respondents indicated a low perception to expertise requests with networking. Expertise requests was ranked as the seventh of the nine perceived benefits as reported by the interviewed entrepreneurs. Baker (2000) suggests that becoming a 'network builder' is a critical part of providing expertise to the shared network, and that seasoned entrepreneurs who take charge of such situations are more likely to be successful when they attend to the network-building responsibilities. The response of the entrepreneurs demonstrated a low perceived value of using the established business network as a tool to gain expertise requests into areas where the entrepreneur lacked information, knowledge and/or experience.

4.2.4 Stay Connected

The next issue which was explored was the perceived importance of using the network for Staying Connected. The overall score for Staying Connected was 1.6 out of 5.0, with six scoring as Strongly Agree (Entrepreneurs 2, 4, 6, 7, 8 and 9), two as Agree (Entrepreneurs 1 and 5) and two scoring as Neutral (Entrepreneurs 3 and 10). Table 4.6 illustrates the responses of the entrepreneurs, indicating the perceived value of Staying Connected as very important to networking.

Stay Connected	16				
	Strongly Agree	Agree	Neutral	Disagree	Strongly Disagree
Entrepreneur 1		x			
Entrepreneur 2	x				
Entrepreneur 3			x		
Entrepreneur 4	x				
Entrepreneur 5		x			
Entrepreneur 6	x				
Entrepreneur 7	x				
Entrepreneur 8	x				
Entrepreneur 9	x				
Entrepreneur 10			x		

Table 4.6: Staying Connected

When asked about the importance of staying connected, Entrepreneur 2 suggested,

> "Absolutely-- without a doubt --staying connected is important to me. The more you know somebody the more you can help them in terms of what they need to be successful from working with them, helping them through something you've gone through or making an important introduction. At the end of the day, I want to help other entrepreneurs go places."

One of the most widely used functions of LinkedIn as reported in the research interviews was the weekly contact update email. A number of entrepreneurs reported reading the weekly LinkedIn email. Some entrepreneurs reported that it was because of the updates within the email that prompted a follow-up email sent directly to the connection (as congratulations, a suggestion of a resource, or any other reason to make contact with the connection). Entrepreneur 5 explained that they read the weekly LinkedIn email in order to stay connected with their network, as it helps to assess the recent happenings of various connections, as well as encourages the entrepreneur to contact connections and stay on their connections "radar screen". Entrepreneur 7 also views the email update as a useful tool, as they reported that, even though an active user, they tend to be reactive within their network.

In summary, the perceived benefit of networking related to staying connected with regard to this research would suggest that the respondents indicated a high perception of staying connected through networking. Staying connected was ranked as the second of the nine perceived benefits as reported by the interviewed entrepreneurs. This high- perceived value of networking would suggest alignment with other research indicating that a solid network of good relationships leads to happiness, satisfaction and a meaningful life (Baker, 2000).

4.2.5 Future Business Opportunity

The next issue which was explored was the perceived importance of using the network for Future Business Opportunity. The overall score for Future Business Opportunity was 1.5 out of 5.0, with six scoring as Strongly Agree (Entrepreneurs 2, 4, 5, 6, 9 and 10), three as Agree (Entrepreneurs 1, 3 and 8) and with one of the ten entrepreneurs (Entrepreneur 7) scoring this perceived benefit as Neutral. Table 4.7 illustrates the responses of the entrepreneurs, indicating the perceived value of Future Business Opportunity as very important to networking.

Future Business Opportunity	1.5				
	Strongly Agree	Agree	Neutral	Disagree	Strongly Disagree
Entrepreneur 1		x			
Entrepreneur 2	x				
Entrepreneur 3		x			
Entrepreneur 4	x				
Entrepreneur 5	x				
Entrepreneur 6	x				
Entrepreneur 7			x		
Entrepreneur 8		x			
Entrepreneur 9	x				
Entrepreneur 10	x				

Table 4.7: Future Business Opportunity

Entrepreneur 4 sees value in finding future business opportunities outside of Ireland:

> "I have a lot of LinkedIn connections in Ireland, people I know through conferences or who I've done some business with in the past. When I started on LinkedIn it was kind of more explicit reason of trying to find people outside of Ireland and specifically because LinkedIn being an American company, we'd be able to find some good people in the US markets. It has made it easier to connect with the right people. If I want to find someone within AT&T, or if I want to find someone in a government department, it is now much easier to do using my network rather than digging through websites and contact lists to find the link. So it has definitely been good from that perspective."

Similarly, other entrepreneurs perceived value in finding Future Business Opportunities. For example, Entrepreneur 9 reported a benefit for future business opportunities in the international market through networking, particularly by allowing advertisement of specific skills (e.g., linguistic abilities).

In summary, the perceived benefit of networking related to future business opportunity with regard to this research would suggest that the respondents indicated a high perception of future through business opportunity networking. This score is consistent with networking research by Baker (2000) that suggests "over four thousand empirical studies that document the prominent role of social networks in the diffusion or spread of products and services."

4.2.6 Partnership Opportunity

The next issue which was explored was the perceived importance of using the network for Partnership Opportunity. The overall score for Partnership Opportunity was 1.8 out of 5.0, with four of the ten entrepreneurs (Entrepreneurs 2, 4, 5 and 10) scoring this perceived benefit as Strongly Agree, four as Agree (Entrepreneurs 1, 3, 6 and 8) and two as Neutral (Entrepreneurs 7 and 9). Table 4.8 illustrates the responses of the entrepreneurs, indicating the perceived value of Partnership Opportunity as important to networking.

Partnership Opportunity	1.8				
	Strongly Agree	Agree	Neutral	Disagree	Strongly Disagree
Entrepreneur 1		x			
Entrepreneur 2	x				
Entrepreneur 3		x			
Entrepreneur 4	x				
Entrepreneur 5	x				
Entrepreneur 6		x			
Entrepreneur 7			x		
Entrepreneur 8		x			
Entrepreneur 9			x		
Entrepreneur 10	x				

Table 4.8: Partnership Opportunity

Partnership Opportunity scored high on the scale; those that use LinkedIn for the purpose find the service to be effective. Entrepreneur 1 reported:

> "I look at the updates to the network on my homepage, the industry news, my connection updates and the quick headlines on some of the groups. I've been able to tailor my site to show me specific partnership opportunities. When I see a possible partnership, I do a little research and then attempt to make the introduction for a connection."

Entrepreneur 8 was interested in social entrepreneurship and used the LinkedIn network to find contacts and partnership opportunities in the area. As a result of this proactive networking, he is now seen as an expert in the field and has had a number of partnership opportunity requests within the specialized industry.

Entrepreneur 7 was able to arrange a number of speakers from their LinkedIn network with industry peers they had met before but either lost contact details or forgot about. The LinkedIn network provided updated contact information and the connection was re-established with a simple email.

In summary, the perceived benefit of networking related to partnership opportunity with regard to this research would suggest that the respondents indicated a high perception of partnership opportunity through networking. Staying connected was ranked as the third of the nine perceived benefits as reported by the interviewed entrepreneurs. This high perception is in contrast with literature review by Baker (2000), "…as compatible alliance partners often find each other via their social and business contacts."

4.2.7 Personal Networking

The next issue which was explored was the perceived importance of using the network for Personal Networking. The overall score for Personal Networking was 2.2 out of 5.0, with two of the ten entrepreneurs (Entrepreneur 2 and 6) scoring this perceived benefit as Strongly Agree, five as Agree (Entrepreneurs 1, 4, 7, 8 and 9), two (Entrepreneurs 3 and 10) as Neutral and one as Disagree (Entrepreneur 5). Table 4.9 illustrates the responses of the entrepreneurs, indicating the perceived value of Personal Networking as important to networking.

Some of the entrepreneurs reported active use with other social networking services such as Facebook and Twitter. However, the overall consensus was that LinkedIn was for business purposes while Facebook was used more for personal connections. Entrepreneur 3 stated:

> "…LinkedIn is slightly different to some of the more traditional social networking models. Facebook is very social, as is Twitter, but LinkedIn is more business focused. You can actually connect with people that have more meaning behind them, decision makers. Not just the everyday folks you know."

Personal Networking	2.2				
	Strongly Agree	Agree	Neutral	Disagree	Strongly Disagree
Entrepreneur 1		x			
Entrepreneur 2	x				
Entrepreneur 3			x		
Entrepreneur 4		x			
Entrepreneur 5				x	
Entrepreneur 6	x				
Entrepreneur 7		x			
Entrepreneur 8		x			
Entrepreneur 9		x			
Entrepreneur 10			x		

Table 4.9: Personal Networking

However, some entrepreneurs also noted that personal networking plays an important role as well, providing examples of how it is a useful way of interacting with both personal friends and business acquaintances.

In summary, the perceived benefit of networking related to personal networking with regard to this research would suggest that the respondents indicated a moderate perception of personal networking through networking. Personal networking was ranked as the fifth of the nine perceived benefits as reported by the interviewed entrepreneurs. Hirsch (1981, p. 169) supports this moderate perception as "social networks involve far more than provision of narrow categories of help as networks reflect the nature and value of our participation in the major life spheres."

4.2.8 Research

The next issue which was explored was the perceived importance of using the network for Research. The overall score for Research was 1.9 out of 5.0, with four of the ten entrepreneurs (Entrepreneurs 2, 3, 5 and 8) scoring this perceived benefit as Strongly Agree, four (Entrepreneur 1, 4, 6 and 9) as Agree, one (Entrepreneur 10) as neutral and one (Entrepreneur 7) as Disagree. Table 4.10 illustrates the responses of the entrepreneurs, indicating the perceived value of Research as very important to networking.

Entrepreneur 5 explained how they use LinkedIn for business research:

> "I like the ability to see the history of some individual where you'd never have known that previously. I suppose if you were to believe everything on LinkedIn then it can add credibility to an individual. In addition to looking at their profile, I look at their recommendations they have received from others and particularly recommendations from those people that I

personally know. That builds a level of credibility to that individual, so there is a trust element that you develop because of it."

Research	1.9				
	Strongly Agree	Agree	Neutral	Disagree	Strongly Disagree
Entrepreneur 1		x			
Entrepreneur 2	x				
Entrepreneur 3	x				
Entrepreneur 4		x			
Entrepreneur 5	x				
Entrepreneur 6		x			
Entrepreneur 7				x	
Entrepreneur 8	x				
Entrepreneur 9		x			
Entrepreneur 10			x		

Table 4.10: Research

The remaining entrepreneurs used LinkedIn for different types of research. For example, Entrepreneur 3 found that using LinkedIn made the initial connection with a potential client easier as it made information about people more accessible. Entrepreneur 8 also used LinkedIn to fulfill research purposes, as they found that exposure fostered by LinkedIn helped in the development of their own research interests. Finally, Entrepreneur 7 pointed out that LinkedIn can be useful when travelling, as they used LinkedIn to see if any of their connections were in the area being visited.

In summary, the perceived benefit of networking related to research with regard to this research would suggest that the respondents indicated a moderate perception of research through networking. Research was ranked as the fourth of the nine perceived benefits as reported by the interviewed entrepreneurs. An example of using a network for research includes, but is not limited to, an entrepreneur using a business relationship with bankers within the business network to arrange financing at a lower interest rate as compared with other entrepreneurs that maintain an 'arm's-length' relationship with a bank. It is through the research and the business network that entrepreneurs are able to provide the needed funding for growth.

4.2.9 Sales Prospecting

The ninth issue which was explored was the perceived importance of using the network for Sales Prospecting. The overall score for Sales Prospecting was 2.6 out of 5.0 with three of the ten entrepreneurs (Entrepreneurs 5, 6 and 10) scoring this perceived benefit as Strongly Agree, two

(Entrepreneurs 3 and 4) as Agree, two (Entrepreneurs 1 and 9) as Neutral, two (Entrepreneurs 7 and 8) as Disagree and one (Entrepreneur 2) as Strongly Disagree. Table 4.11 illustrates the responses of the entrepreneurs, indicating the perceived value of Sales Prospecting as important to networking.

Sales Prospecting	2.6				
	Strongly Agree	Agree	Neutral	Disagree	Strongly Disagree
Entrepreneur 1			x		
Entrepreneur 2					x
Entrepreneur 3		x			
Entrepreneur 4		x			
Entrepreneur 5	x				
Entrepreneur 6	x				
Entrepreneur 7				x	
Entrepreneur 8				x	
Entrepreneur 9			x		
Entrepreneur 10	x				

Table 4.11: Sales Prospecting

Entrepreneur 10 shared how he uses his LinkedIn network for sales prospecting:

> "I've begun to use LinkedIn more over the past six months. I use it primarily from new business point of view. I find that it is an excellent way to approach a potential sponsor on behalf of my clients rather than sending a generic cold-call type email to info@ or marketing@ brand.com. I can actually search on LinkedIn for a particular company to see if there is anyone within my network who works within the company, approach them directly through in-mail or by being part of the similar LinkedIn group and begin to lay the foundation for a future relationship. These things take time."

Other entrepreneurs also reported using LinkedIn as part of their sales process, ranging from merely planning to generate business using their network to checking potential customers' information through their LinkedIn profiles.

In summary, the perceived benefit of networking related to sales prospecting with regard to this research would suggest that the respondents indicated a low perception of sales prospecting through networking. Sales prospecting was ranked as the eighth of the nine perceived benefits as reported by the interviewed entrepreneurs. The use of the network for sales prospecting boosts business performance as entrepreneurs that use the network can have access to business information, word of mouth marketing and a shorter sales cycle by allowing customers to conduct business with others already part of the network.

4.2.10 Summary for Research Objective One

Research Objective One explored the perceived benefits of networking by Irish entrepreneurs sampled. The primary data identified three main perceived benefits of social networking as future business opportunity, staying connected and partnership opportunity. The primary data also illustrated that the lowest three ranked perceived benefits were career opportunities, sales prospecting and expertise requests. The second research objective will analyse the formation, maintenance and development of entrepreneurial networks.

4.3 Analysis of Objective Two: The formation, development and maintenance of entrepreneurial networks

The second research objective of this research established the formation, development and maintenance of entrepreneurial networks. LinkedIn's philosophy states that a person's professional relationships are the key to professional success:

> "Your professional network of trusted contacts gives you an advantage in your career, and is one of your most valuable assets. LinkedIn exists to help you make better use of your professional network and help the people you trust in return. Our mission is to connect the world's professionals to make them more productive and successful. We believe that in a global connected economy, your success as a professional and your competitiveness as a company depend upon faster access to insight and resources you can trust." (LinkedIn, 2009)

Details and additional information are available at <www.linkedin.com>. The data analysis suggests that many of the entrepreneurs interviewed for this research would support this assumption. As presented in Chapter 2, the idea of creating a business network in order to activate the network to achieve business success has become increasingly popular in the business world (Olsen, 2008). There has been an expansion of professional networking services such as LinkedIn (see appendix for LinkedIn annual growth chart).

4.3.1 Formation and Development of Entrepreneurial Networks

Entrepreneurs reported that the use of LinkedIn has changed how networking takes place within a business. Entrepreneur 6 explained their new "networking flow chart" with LinkedIn as the main hub for activity. After attending a networking event and collecting business cards, the Entrepreneur checks to see if the new connection is a member of LinkedIn. If the connection is not a member of LinkedIn, those names are added to a master database for later marketing. However, if the new connection is on LinkedIn, the Entrepreneur will review the profile and connections to establish if there might be potential business synergies. If there is, the Entrepreneur will arrange for a coffee meeting. If there is not an immediate synergy, the new connection will be saved as part of the LinkedIn network for scheduled business updates. Entrepreneur 6 suggested that this networking flowchart has created value to their own networking efforts and has systematized how the entire company now manages the business network.

Similarly, Entrepreneur 3 uses LinkedIn as part of their networking strategy:

> "After I meet a person or get their business card, I follow up with them via LinkedIn.

Entrepreneur 1 explained how others connect with them using LinkedIn:

> "... of the direct invites I've received from LinkedIn, it has been a very small number of direct approaches from people that would have invited me to join their network... really those invites were primarily for, 'can we hope to meet up or can we meet up for a coffee', but nothing really has come out at this point in time."

In summary, it is through the use of social networking services such as LinkedIn that allows entrepreneurs to use the service as a tool that changed how to develop, manage and maintain a business network.

4.3.2 Active versus Passive Networking

The first variable which was explored in order to answer this research question was the style of networking used by Irish entrepreneurs – Active versus Passive. An active networker is one that is interested in having as many connections as possible and accomplishes this goal by sending out invitations to connect, as well as uses the search function within LinkedIn to seek new connections and reviews the connections of connections in order to expand their own network. A passive networker is one that does not spend much time searching for new connections or sending out invitations to connect. The passive networker may log onto LinkedIn to update their profile or get updates on the network, but generally does not bother with network growth. The types of the networkers are based upon the entrepreneur's behavioural pattern as identified in the interview.

The data analysis also suggests that an individual's reaction towards networking can change based upon what is needed by the networker at that particular point in time. For example, an entrepreneur that has a new product or service will tend to be more active in their networking activities than when the product or service is in the development stage. Networkers who were in need of additional resources or who were connected with other networkers that valued professional networking also tended to be active networkers. Those within smaller networks or those who were content with the resources currently available to them tended to be more passive in their network creation.

All of the entrepreneurs reported a score of Agree or higher in knowing their connections better by using LinkedIn. Even though an entrepreneur reported 'knowing' their connections better through the use of LinkedIn, these same entrepreneurs maintained a professional and business relationship with the connections.

For many entrepreneurs, the use of technology to manage and connect with their network does not replace the face-to-face interactions that can often lead to friendship. The research in Chapter 2 introduced the term " e-quaintance". Fraser (2008) defines an e-quaintance as an online friend. Other definitions include:

> "...typically a 'friend' within a website or online setting exclusively; which ironically don't allow for the depth of interaction, rapport and social connection that friends of a conventional nature share." (Urban Dictionary, 2009)

One of the observations from the analysis of the data was that many of the entrepreneurs who were identified as passive networkers also suggested that they sought to make new connections.

Entrepreneur 2 explained:

> "Initially it would have been others looking for me; now it's me being more active, me looking for other people, people that I have met and I want to maintain some kind of professional relationship with. I really have a vague idea of them and want to re-establish professional contact with them. So I search for them."

Entrepreneur 2 echoed a common statement for the desire for a well-established network with a goal to have a network of strong ties.

Entrepreneur 6 desired quality over quantity:

> "I don't see a point in having hundreds and hundreds of connections. If I don't know them and if we can't do business together, then what is the point of a connection? So I'd definitely go for quality over quantity."

The data analysis shows a split with regard to an explanation of e-quaintances in the research of Irish entrepreneurs. When asked to evaluate the statement, "The people I am connected with through my social network are people I would consider true friends", the overall score of the statement was 3.6 out of 5.0, with two of the entrepreneurs showing agreement (Entrepreneurs 4 and 7), three with a neutral response (Entrepreneurs 1, 3 and 10), five reporting disagreement (Entrepreneurs 2 and 8) and three strong disagreements (Entrepreneurs 5, Entrepreneur 6, Entrepreneur 9). These results are displayed in the following graph and would support the fact that for the Irish entrepreneur, online networking is different than creating a friendship.

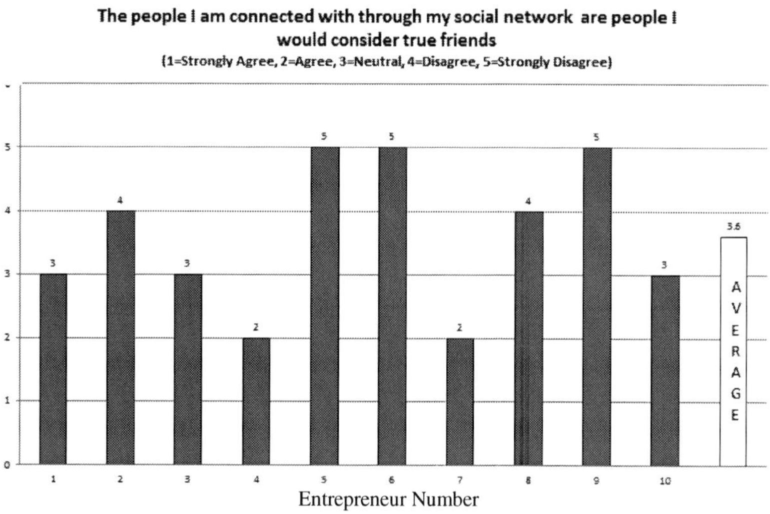

Figure 4.1: Social network friendship

When asked to evaluate the statement "I have become friends with people I would otherwise not know through my social network", the average response was 2.4 out of 5.0 with four Strongly Agree responses

(Entrepreneurs 2, 3, 4 and 10), two Agree responses (Entrepreneurs 5 and 6), one Neutral response (Entrepreneur 1), two Disagree responses (Entrepreneurs 7 and 8) and one Strongly Disagree (Entrepreneur 9) response. These results are displayed in the graph below.

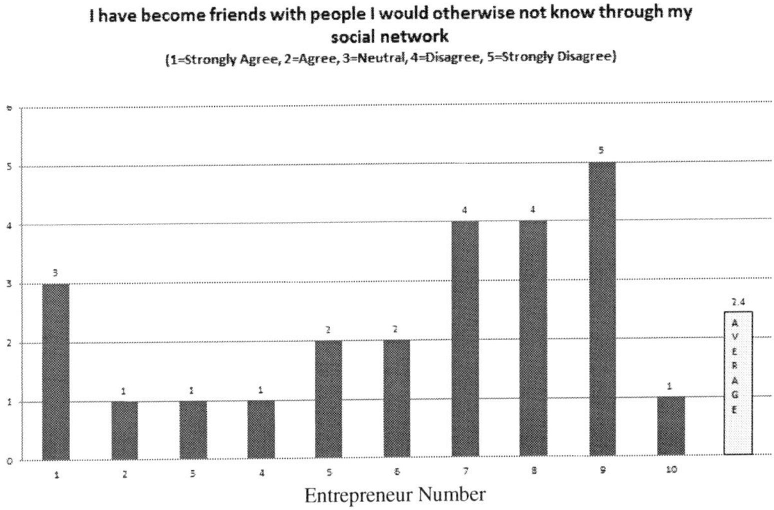

Figure 4.2: Friendship through social network

The data also suggest that while entrepreneurs understand the value of online social networking, 60% of the entrepreneurs see it as simply a means to an end.

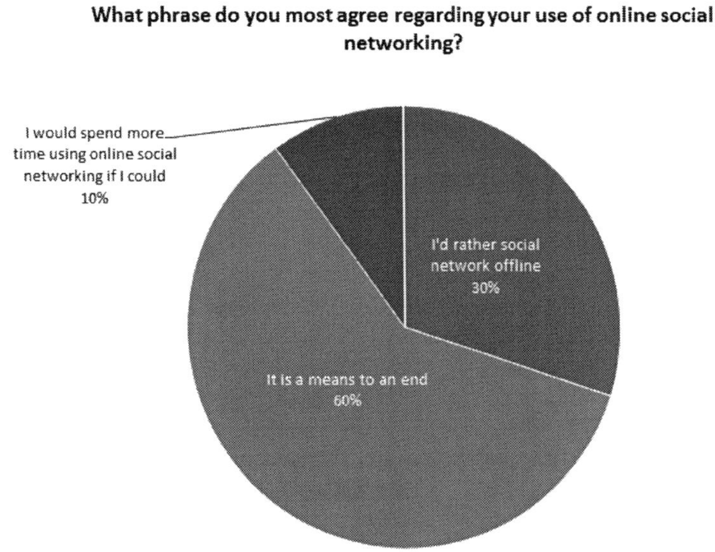

Figure 4.3: Use of online social networking

When asked, "I feel like I know my connections better because of LinkedIn", all entrepreneurs scored the statement as either Strongly Agree (six entrepreneurs) or Agree (four entrepreneurs), as illustrated below.

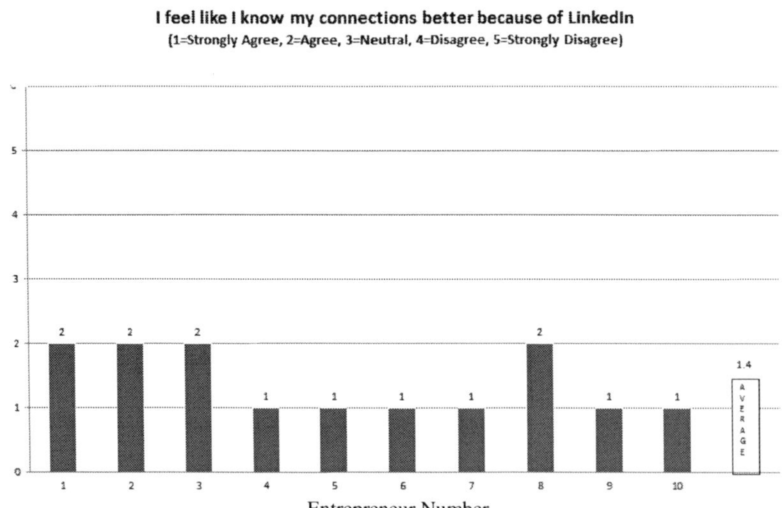

Figure 4.4: Familiarity with LinkedIn connections

4.3.3 Open Networking versus Closed Networking

The second variable which was explored in order to answer this research question was the strategy used by Irish entrepreneurs with regards to networking. Regardless of the type of network, two networking strategies became apparent as to how the entrepreneurs developed their own network. These strategies were defined as either being Open or Closed networks and relate directly to how entrepreneurs form, develop and maintain their networks. Based on the definition given in Chapter 2, it was determined that the overall group favoured a Closed network.

There are both positive and negative aspects to both the Open and Closed networking strategies. In an Open networking strategy, there is a perceived benefit in being able to connect with as many connections as possible over different industries and on a global basis. As discussed in the previous chapter, this "weak tie" approach has been identified as important with regard to where a person will find future opportunity and access to new resources. A networker that tends to be at the extreme range of open networking on LinkedIn is called a "lion". These networkers will connect with anyone and often market themselves as a "lion" within their own profile. None of the entrepreneurs in this research study identified themselves as a LinkedIn lion. In an Open networking strategy, where a person is connecting with as many people as possible, there can be a perceived weakness in the strength of the network as the connections may not know each other on a more personal level.

While the majority of the entrepreneurs would be classified as closed networkers who possessed a strong desire for quality of network versus quantity of network, there was a noticeable increase in each entrepreneur's number of connections over a three-month period. All entrepreneurs except one showed an increase in the number of connections. The entrepreneur in question purged his network after participation in the research after realizing the importance of a smaller network, thus causing a -22% change in the size of the network. Overall, the group experienced a 27% increase in the size of the overall network. Three of the entrepreneurs experienced a greater than 50% increase in network size.

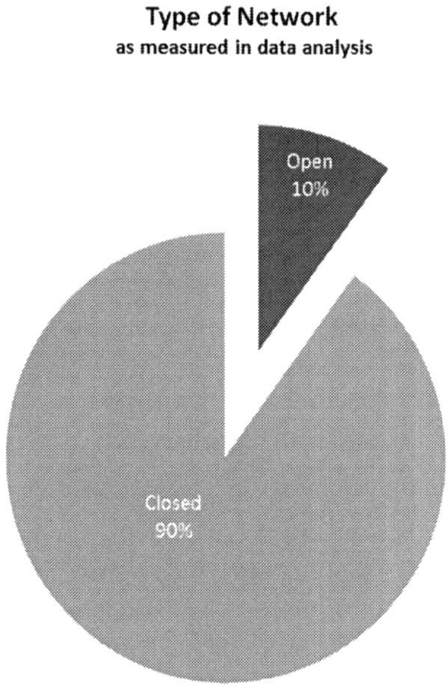

Figure 4.5: Type of network

Quality over quantity was a common trend among the entrepreneurs. In addition, a mutually beneficial network was important to Entrepreneur 2:

> "…my connecting with others is very concrete. It is with people that I have met and with whom I think [that] can be of mutual benefit."

Entrepreneur 7 suggested the importance of knowing each person in the network on a more personal level, preferring a strong but small network. Entrepreneur 10 added that for a network to be of value, it needs to be one where all parties within the network can be vulnerable and can ask for help:

> "I just read a business article that pretty much sums up what I think a network is about. The author said when 'I judge the value of my network, it's not by how many people are in my rolodex. It's by how many people I can pick up the phone to call and say, "I need help" – and by how many of them would call me to say the same'."

Entrepreneur 10 was the one entrepreneur that was identified as an Open Networker:

> "…for me it's much more about quality than quantity. Now having said that, I know for a fact that I have connected with people who I've no prior experience dealing with. I regularly get invitations to connect, but before I do, I view their profile. If I feel the person has relevance to my industry, I'll approach them and say to them that I am more than happy to chat even though we haven't met in person or had any kind of business dealings."

Entrepreneur 7 shared a concern with not being able to be fully engaged with the network:

> "I want to be able to give my network 100% of my time when I am engaged with them, thus I keep my network small and personal and I suppose that's why I don't interact with LinkedIn as much as I should because if I do it means my time is being given away and it doesn't necessarily give me bonds and receipts for records or it does give me something that is maybe a guest speaker that I'll need in September."

The quality of the relationship in the network was an important factor for many entrepreneurs. When asked about quantity over quality, the results were in favour of the quality of the connections rather than quantity of connections.

Entrepreneur 2:

> "Quality of the connections is more important to me than the total number of connections. I have deliberately not connected with everybody that I know is on LinkedIn. I connect with people that are useful to me that I can be of use to."

Other entrepreneurs voiced similar opinions. For example, Entrepreneur 4 indicated that the quality of connections was important to personal credibility. Similarly, Entrepreneur 3 refrained from engaging business connections with personal updates to maintain the quality of the relationship.

Many of the entrepreneurs identified with closed networking. Entrepreneur 1 explained:

> "...I tend to be selective with whom I invite into my network. If I get an email that is completely out of left field, where I can't figure out why this person is contacting me, I will decline. But if I can see there might be some sort of common interest, I will follow-up. But if it is obvious that it is junk mail like the kind you get from Skype -- for example, from these places in China just wanting to meet up and wire money into my bank account -- then absolutely I'd decline that."

Entrepreneur 3 suggested a network where potential business was the main goal:

> "For me, strong ties are those whom I've actually dealt with or done some business with in the past. Then there are the in-between ties, those that we haven't done business [with] but there is a strong potential, and then the people you know you are probably not going to do business with and they are in the same space as you are."

Entrepreneur 8 shared a perspective that identified a potential reason for a closed networking approach:

> "For any person from a business and research point of view, a smaller focused network is better because I feel I can monitor and control it and maintain regular contact. I think there is a point that if you connect to just anybody then it becomes very much you know you are being bombarded by information, contact's emails and I think it's very hard to decide who is better so keep focus and manageable at the moment."

Entrepreneur 5 uses a closed approach within LinkedIn:

> "I find connections on LinkedIn predominantly through the listing that is provided in terms of companies that I have been related to in the past as an employee or whatever else, or through the suggestions and 'The people you may know' prompt box. Other ways are through personal communication or contact with people that you meet on a daily basis that you may not have met previously and subsequently linking with them."

A trait of a closed network is the desire to know those within the network. Entrepreneur 1 explained that some connections were not known personally, but rather introduced or gathered because of a common interest.

Figure 4.6: Identify yourself

The closed nature of the Irish entrepreneur throughout the research was evident with a number of common traits. Entrepreneur 8 replied:

> "At the moment people are connecting with me and that is really how my network develops - others contacting me. The criteria would be first a relevant area of either research or business. I've kept them quite broad.

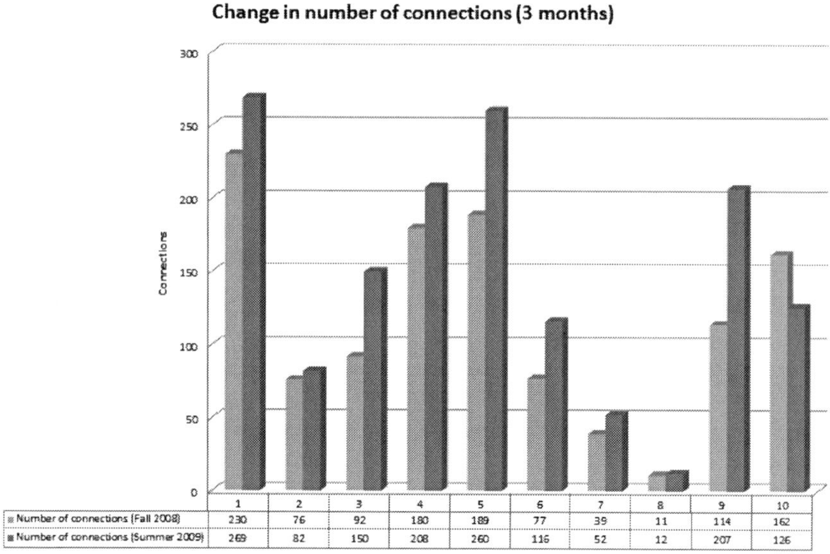

Figure 4.7: Change in number of connections

4.3.4 Summary

Research Objective Two analysed the formation and development of entrepreneurial networks. The primary data identified that Irish entrepreneurs fall into one of two types of networking – Active or Passive -- and either one of two methods of networking – Open or Closed. The data suggest that 90% of the entrepreneurs in this research study would be considered Active Closed networkers.

The third research objective will analyse the use of technology to manage social capital.

4.4 Analysis of Objective Three: The use of technology to manage social capital

The entrepreneur's previous experience using technology to manage their network and thus their social capital in conjunction with their keen interest in the management of said network reflects the fact that most of the entrepreneurs understood the importance of a professional business network prior to joining LinkedIn.

Although LinkedIn was seen as especially useful in relation to the management of weak ties, it also provided contributions to the management of strong ties. The variation of strong ties and weak ties that are represented through LinkedIn has led to the identification of three main functions of LinkedIn (Olsen, 2008). These include:

1. Symbol of a connection: the connection functioned as a representation of a tie that already existed.
2. Re-establishment of connections: connections that for various reasons had been lost were re-established when connected through LinkedIn.
3. Constitution of connections: new connections were constituted as a result of disclosure on LinkedIn.

The first function is that of LinkedIn as a symbol of a connection. Many of the connections supported through LinkedIn were between previously established ties that already had certain patterns of communication. The connection through LinkedIn functioned as a representation of a tie that already existed. As such, LinkedIn did not function as the primary form of communication, and instead became a supplement to existing forms. This symbol was especially apparent in relation to strong ties, as the relationships are generally maintained through several different mediums of communication (Garton et al., 1997; Haythornthwaite, 2000).

The second function is that LinkedIn supports the re-establishment of connections. For many different reasons, both strong ties and weak ties that had been lost were re-established because of the connection through LinkedIn. In such instances LinkedIn functioned as the initial form of communication, but was often supplemented with other forms of communication, such as email or telephone, depending on the desire to interact. This function was generally represented through various weak ties with former classmates or past work colleagues.

The third function is that LinkedIn supports the constitution of a connection. The literature review suggests that in such cases it is through LinkedIn that the connection is created, as well as maintained. Most of these relationships are weak ties.

These three functions may also support the three tasks that Nardi et al. (2002) presented in previous literature as necessary to build a successful professional network:

- The constitution of connections adds new resources to the professional network and helps to build the network;

- The re-establishment of connections assists in building the professional network, as resources that may have been lost are reconstituted;
- The symbol of a connection contributes to the maintenance of both strong and weak ties, as it functions as a representation of ties that already exist, and makes the connections more visible to the entire network.

These functions supported both strong and weak ties, although some were more beneficial to one member or the other.

Entrepreneur 6 explained:

> "I try to engage with everyone in my network every four to six months. I have switched to using LinkedIn as follow up with some of my connections on a weekly basis. I've found that LinkedIn is a great tool to follow up so they don't forget that they've met you. Without them remembering who you are, then networking events become totally ineffective. LinkedIn is actually helping our offline networking."

Entrepreneur 3 noted:

> "... for those that I have been in contact with before and I have built offline relationships by sharing different networking events, conferences or I've met in person, that I guess that's solidified the actual business relationship as a whole."

A majority of the entrepreneurs agreed or strongly agreed that through LinkedIn, re-establishment of a connection has occurred.

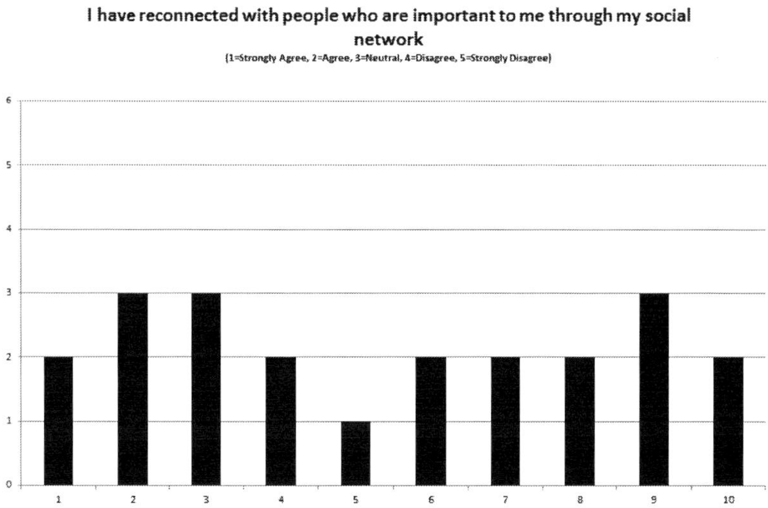

Figure 4.8: Reconnected with people through social networking

Entrepreneur 6 shared:

> "LinkedIn has changed how we do business. Our industry is so vulnerable in Ireland that we find it very important to have access to experts, and LinkedIn helps with that. We have adopted American and even European models but ours would be the first business of its kind operating in Ireland, which means we need more exposure because not only our company is unknown, but our concept and what we do is unknown in Ireland and that's why online is hugely important to us. This is the first time we really got to work so even I'm hoping that by next year we'll be far more effective."

The importance of a tool to maintain the network was evident with a majority of the entrepreneurs. When asked if they would have lost contact with their connections, nine out of ten entrepreneurs agreed or strongly agreed with the statement.

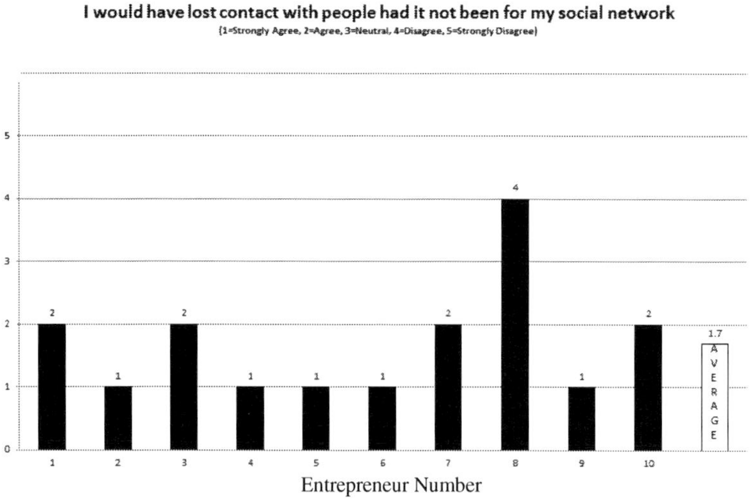

Figure 4.9: Maintained contact through social networking

When asked about the use of technology within business, the majority of entrepreneurs reported to be "early majority" with regards to technology innovation:

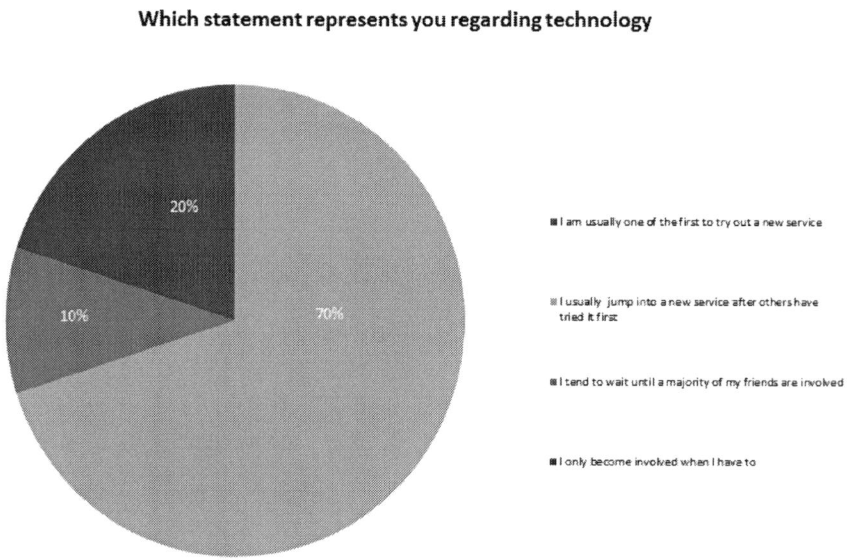

Figure 4.10: Relationship with technology

For some, the decision to use technology to manage social capital was a reaction rather than a conscious decision. Entrepreneur 2 reported:

> "I joined LinkedIn after a co-worker invited me. Just to keep him happy I just said "Yes, I accept". Then all of sudden I started getting invitations from people that I knew who were on LinkedIn telling me how great the site was. I must admit, my use of it in the first year was pretty passive. Since then I've been quite active."

The decision on which technology to use to manage the network depends on the dynamics of the network. Entrepreneur 8 stated:

> "How I connect with a group depends on who the group is. If I am working with female entrepreneurs with a less technical background, I might talk about non-technical methods of networking or email. For larger groups, we would use LinkedIn or Plaxo to maintain connection because these are the sites they are familiar with."

One of the benefits reported by the entrepreneurs was the ability to have one central location for the entire network, allowing easy access to both the personal and professional network.

Entrepreneur 2 explained:

> "I have a mix of people in my network. I'd say about a third of the people have been a part of my life at some stage before. They could be entrepreneurs, could be academics, quite a mix there. One third would be co-workers and newer connections and the last third friends."

The ease of use with technology to manage the network was highlighted by Entrepreneur 8:

> "There are preconceived ideas about social networking sites and people think it is more complicated than it actually is. I try to demystify the whole process. If I'm doing a workshop with particular individuals who may not be technically savvy, I will show that you don't need to be a hi-tech person; you should be able to avail of this kind of connectivity."

The following table highlights how the entrepreneurs communicate with the network over the course of time. Of particular interest are the daily use of technology (mobile phone, email and LinkedIn) and the less frequent use of what can be considered a less technological method – postal mail.

Entrepreneur 10 explained the financial and time difference in using technology:

> "..if it was a case that I was going to connect with my contacts by postal mail and wanted to meet everyone in person, then the number of new business opportunities that would be open to me would be less than present, so from that point of view the technology is very helpful and important to my business. I think also because of my age, my generation uses technology more. I have peers that use Twitter, Facebook and all those kind of social networking sites. I [have] become very used to using the internet to run both my work life and my social life."

Different websites cater to different market segments. As a professional, Entrepreneur 7 identified with LinkedIn over other social networking services:

> "…I'm with Facebook, I'm not with Bebo. Bebo, I consider it for young kids, and Twitter I haven't yet tried. So my first allegiance would be to LinkedIn because it has an element of professionalism I'm looking for."

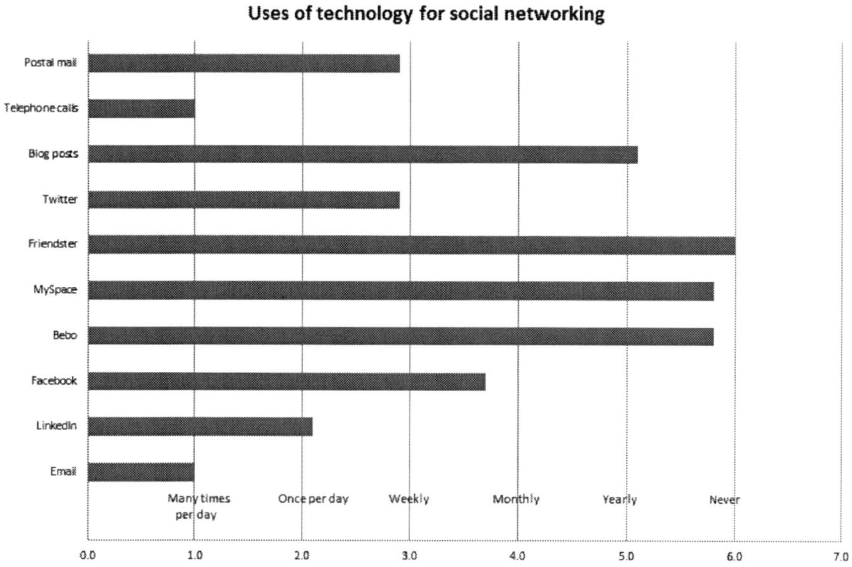

Figure 4.11: Uses of technology for social networking

Entrepreneurs also indicated the importance of having a professional and personal online presence and the desire not to mix the two.

Entrepreneur 3 suggested:

> "… for me, my Twitter and Facebook are quite social networks. My LinkedIn is more for business. Being able to separate the business from pleasure networks in my mind does give more credibility.

Entrepreneur 10 explained:

> "I think it would be impossible to regulate avoiding spammers. I do question the value of having people on thousands -- if not tens of thousands -- of connections. I wonder about the value of that. On Facebook I have friends who have a thousand friends and I'm sure they are not all close friends. As long as you are creative enough about how to use it I don't see any negativity."

When asked about their use of technology, all entrepreneurs reported an increase in the overall use of technology in business. All entrepreneurs also reported an increased desire to network with connections compared to five years ago.

The importance of a business network and the associated social capital is directly related to the success of the entrepreneur. When asked to gauge how a business network is related to success, six of the ten entrepreneurs gave a percentage score of 50% or higher when asked to provide an overall score.

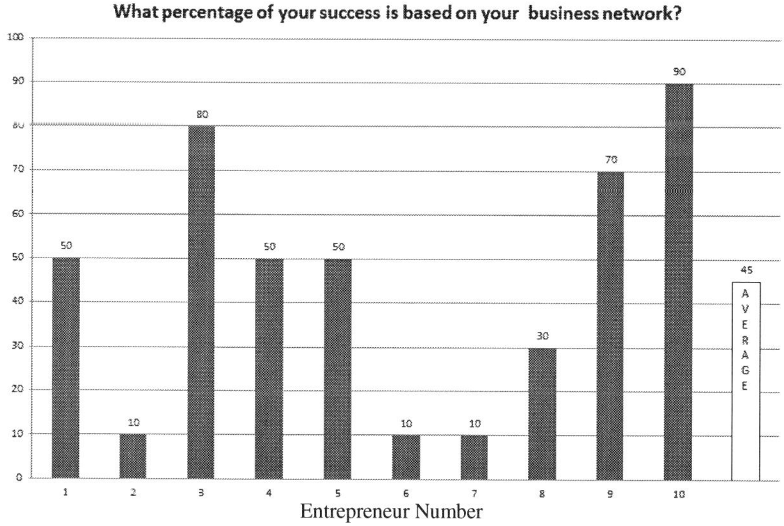

Figure 4.12: Percentage of success based on business network

4.5 Conclusion

In achieving Research Objective One, the perceived benefits of networking were explored. From the collection and analysis of the primary data, it was established that different entrepreneurs network for different reasons, depending on the immediate needs of the entrepreneur.

Research Objective Two investigated how an Irish entrepreneur forms, develops and maintains a business network. The empirical data suggest that while there are a number of different tools available to form, develop and maintain a business network, social networking services, such as LinkedIn, are growing in use throughout Ireland.

Research Objective Three reviewed how technology was used to manage a business network and thus the social capital of an entrepreneur. All entrepreneurs suggested an increase in the use of technology in their businesses and partially attributed their business success directly to the network.

CHAPTER FIVE

DISCUSSION AND CONCLUSION

5.1 Introduction

The purpose of this research was to explore the role of social capital and how Irish entrepreneurs use LinkedIn to develop, maintain and manage their business network. In order to answer this research question, a literature review was conducted on social capital, business network formation and social networking services. The results of empirical research of this study support some of the research on social networking services to develop, maintain and manage a business network, while simultaneously, some findings from this research contradict previous findings on the use of technology to manage the business networking process. In this chapter the findings of each research objective is re-iterated and the results of this research which verify entrepreneurship research to date are presented. Finally, areas of further research are recommended and recommendations for public policy are presented.

This research supports Nardi et al.'s (2002) analysis of professional networking as something that has become part of the overall culture in the social lives of many professionals. This research also emphasizes that professional networking services may act as useful tools when building and managing professional networks. Baker (2000, p. 9) supports this theory, as "success is social: it depends on relationships with others. All the individual ingredients for success – natural talent, intelligence, education, effort and luck – are intricately intertwined within social networks." Analysis of the interviews supports the literature in that social capital was identified as one of the key factors that provide continued success and growth.

Baym et al. (2004) emphasize that entrepreneurs generally employ various business tools when they communicate, and that sites such as LinkedIn usually supplement other forms of communication. Nardi et al. (2002) found that being able to manage a professional network, and the ability to stay updated on those connections, was of great significance to many professionals. In addition, the previous research found that the establishment and maintenance of connections required much effort to make it efficient. Existing technology, such as e-mail, instant messaging, mobile phones and personal digital assistants, was judged as inadequate. At the time of the Nardi et al. (2002) study, professional networking services such as LinkedIn existed, but were not as popular as they are today. The growth of such services indicates that social networking technology may have filled the gap that Nardi et al. (2002) identified.

This research was a qualitative study on how Irish entrepreneurs use technology to manage an entrepreneurial business network and in so doing, social capital. Through the literature review and data analysis, it was identified that there are several different approaches to the perceived benefits of networking, how to create, maintain and develop a network and the use of technology to manage social capital.

This research explores a number of issues in relation to Irish entrepreneurs and the use of technology on networking practices. The research objectives of the research were as follows:

- Research objective one aimed to ascertain the perceived benefits of networking;
- Research objective two explored how the Irish entrepreneur forms, maintains and develops their network;
- Research objective three explored how the Irish entrepreneur uses technology to manage social capital.

Findings from the current research both support and extend previous research. The data is consistent with research regarding how entrepreneurs use technology to form, maintain and develop social capital through a business network, but are inconsistent with previous investigations on social capital. In this chapter, the results of each research objective are revisited and described. In addition, those findings that support the literature concerning entrepreneurship and social capital are presented. The chapter closes with recommendations for future research.

5.2 Conclusion for Research Objective One: The perceived benefits of networking.

In achieving Research Objective One, the perceived benefit of networking of entrepreneurs in Ireland was investigated. The research question was formulated based upon the literature review in Chapter Two, which highlighted the concept of networking in business, access to networking and the motivations for creation of a social network). The perceived benefits of networking as identified in the interviews with Irish entrepreneurs were inconsistent with the literature review. As noted in Chapter 2, (Olsen 2008; Lynch 2009) research suggests a higher perceived value for partnership opportunity, staying connected and future business opportunities. The lower than expected scores for different perceived benefits of social networking may partially be attributed to the amount of trust between the connections. More specifically, a traditional offline connection where the connection is strong versus weak implies a certain level of trust. It is the culture of Irish businesses to do business with those one knows on a personal level. It may take time to create the needed relationship; however, once created, a tool such as LinkedIn can provide the needed support structure to maintain and develop the relationship.

Another possible explanation for the different responses is the "newness" of LinkedIn in Ireland. The Irish culture is one of personal engagement. It is a small, well-connected island as is, where it seems everybody knows everybody, even across age ranges and geographical location. The traditional Irish business customs may have not yet fully adopted the potential power of an online social networking service.

As with any tool, there is a learning curve and an opportunity cost to implement the tool. While simplest to some, the structure and layout to some less technologically inclined entrepreneurs may be a limiting factor of usage.

5.3 Conclusion for Research Objective Two: How the Irish entrepreneur forms, maintains and develops a network

In achieving Research Objective Two, how the Irish entrepreneur forms, maintains and develops a network was explored. The research question was based on the literature in Chapter Two, which explored proactive and reactive networking the benefits of social networking for an entrepreneur and Entrepreneurial user types of LinkedIn. The literature review identified that a networker can be defined as either an Active or Passive networker and use either an Open or Closed networking philosophy. During the data analysis, it became clear that the entrepreneurs used networking for a variety of reasons and functions. A pattern emerged that suggests two main types of networkers on LinkedIn: Active and Passive.

One feature of LinkedIn that the entrepreneurs often discussed regarding maintaining the network was the ability to have an overview and updated access of existing connections, but also the experience of the connected connections. In addition to the overview, many of the entrepreneurs noted that LinkedIn made it easy to stay up-to-date with their connections, especially those without general interactions. For example, one entrepreneur (Entrepreneur 10) noted the importance of the immediate update in demographic information (such as change in employment or email change) of his connections. Prior to LinkedIn, this information would only be available when the connection pushed the information to the network. Another entrepreneur (Entrepreneur 4) commented on the ease of LinkedIn to pull the information such as this from the network and the value of the time saved by having this feature. Several of the entrepreneurs suggested that LinkedIn made the management of the network uncomplicated, effortless and time-saving.

5.4 Conclusion for Research Objective Three: How the Irish entrepreneur uses technology to manage social capital

In achieving Research Objective Three, how the Irish entrepreneur uses technology to manage social capital was explored. The research question was based on the literature in Chapter Two, which explored online social networking services and the use of LinkedIn as a social networking tool. The literature review identified that LinkedIn is one of the many social networking services available to entrepreneurs as a tool for interacting with their network. LinkedIn was characterized as a dynamic and flexible professional application that supported social networking through the establishment and maintenance of connections (Olsen, 2008). The entrepreneurs perceived LinkedIn differently according to how it is used, as either a service, a tool and/or a place (Olsen, 2008). Entrepreneurs identified with LinkedIn as just one of these perceptions or a combination of all aspects.

Online social networking remains a relatively new business tool. In a study of American marketers (Stelzer, 2009), a number of facts about social networking were identified:

- 88% of marketers surveyed use social networking to market their businesses, but 72% have only been doing so for a few months or less;
- It takes time to develop relationships that lead to actual business. However, a large percent of marketers who take the time find great results. For example, 61.62% of marketers who have been using social media for years report it has helped them close business. More than half who spend 16 or more hours per week find the same results;

- Entrepreneurs were 9% more likely than those that work within a business to engage in social networking;
- Sole proprietors are the largest identified group of users that "were just getting underway with social networking" (30.2%), while owners of two- to 100-employee businesses identified as the most experienced (29.3% using social networking for years).

These findings support the empirical data and literature review that social networking is an important piece of the overall marketing structure of an entrepreneurial firm.

Previous research (Baker, 2000) also indicated that there is a growing gap between the need for social capital in a networked society and the ability of individuals to build and use it, as there is an observed disappearance in modern life of 'human moments' – genuine face-to-face interactions. This research also suggests the importance of "small acts of compassion and face-to-face conversation to supplement the modern diet of electronic, at-a-glance communication" (Baker, 2000 p. xiv). Ireland is not just the country of a thousand welcomes but also a country with a business culture dedicated to knowing those with whom they do business on a personal level. Irish social capital flourishes as the members of the network form vast connections, with relationships built upon mutual respect, honour and understanding. The Irish generally conduct business within their own networks, and it can be difficult to break into this network; but once accepted into the circle of trust, referrals will follow. This fact shows the importance of maintaining strong networks within the Irish business culture, yet the hesitancy to use technology to maintain the network.

When a technological innovation such as LinkedIn is introduced, not everyone adopts usage at the same point in time. Rather, there will be a range of adoption from innovators to laggards (Rogers, 2003). With regards to LinkedIn as a professional online social capital tool, the sample set for research can be identified as the early adopters of LinkedIn in Ireland, yet it can also be observed that LinkedIn as a business tool within Ireland has yet to become mainstream. This observation is based upon the Irish cultural business practice of conducting business 'face-to-face'. As access to technology continues to increase throughout Ireland and as the younger generation that has been raised to use technology for everything from downloading music to interacting with friends online, social networking services within businesses will increase.

The data analysis suggested that LinkedIn generally functions as a supplement to other tools, both online and offline, which support professional networking. The entrepreneurs used LinkedIn as a tool for an overview of their connections, access to real time information about the network and the ability to connect with the connections of others within the network. As the entrepreneurs' professional networks changed or developed, LinkedIn became a part of the updating process.

As supported in the data analysis, LinkedIn was seen as a tool that provides support to social capital / network management. LinkedIn facilitated the establishment of connections through gaining access to new resources, particularly useful when establishing weak ties (Olsen, 2008).

5.5 Limitations

When analysing the results of this research, certain limitations need to be explored. No matter how long research takes place, there may be other aspects of the context of that research that were not examined. Additional research methods could have been used to create triangulation where attempts are made to cancel the limitations of one method by the use of another to cross-check the findings (Bryman and Bell, 2007).

- **Geographic ethnic bias**

  With respect to the research objectives, a limitation stems from the strategy used; namely, that the results are founded on interpretation. There may have been confusion with the interview questions based on ethnicity. The basis of the interview questions used for this research was based upon a Norwegian thesis. To avoid this possible limitation, the questions were left to the interpretation of the entrepreneur and were reported within the data analysis accordingly.
- **Sample Size**

  Due to the limitation of time, only a small number of Irish entrepreneurs could be interviewed and analysed. The small sample size and the specificity of the entrepreneurs limit the generalization of the findings. These limits are unavoidable given the time constraints of the research. As part of the research, a limitation of the entrepreneur being a user of LinkedIn was important. By restricting the sample size to users of LinkedIn, the generalization of the results could be limited; however, the non-random sample is consistent with the specific focus and nature of this research. The smaller but focused number of entrepreneurs permits a more detailed exploration of the research questions. It is the exploratory nature of this research not to prove some general proposition, but rather to seek a better understanding of the networking process of Irish entrepreneurs.

5.6 Implications and Recommendations

The attraction of a social networking service such as LinkedIn is that when understood and used effectively, the service becomes a time saving, pro-active, cost-effective business development tool. Online networking does not replace face-to-face networking: it compliments it. The findings of this research can be used for developing government strategies for addressing the needs of business networking for entrepreneurs in Ireland and as a tool to assist the modification of existing support systems. These suggestions are now presented; social network training programmes, global business opportunities and evaluation of existing business networking policy.

5.6.1 Social Network training programmes

This research has established the value of a business network and resulting social capital as important to the success of growing businesses. While important, some users remain passive. A recent survey (Jones, 2009) concluded that only 10% of people registered with social networks were actually active within the network. Nine out of ten people on social networking join the service but do not participate. By this calculation, while LinkedIn suggests 45 million members, only 4.5 million would be active users. Simply signing up for a social networking service is not enough to garner an increase in social capital. If an entrepreneur wants to effectively use a tool such as LinkedIn to increase social capital, then the entrepreneur must put forth the time and effort into learning how to use the service. Signing up for a social networking service and not becoming active on the service and then deciding the service is not effective would be similar to attending a chamber of commerce event, without business cards, standing in a corner and then wondering why the event did not produce networking results.

A study by Sapient Interactive (2009) suggests that low participation in social networking sites is caused by a lack of understanding of how the social networking works. An additional 14% of social networking site members reported that they simply do not know where to start with social networking, while only 9% of respondents reported that "social networking is overrated". Training programmes through enterprise boards and local chamber of commerce events that highlight the value of social networking sites along with additional training that assists entrepreneurs in the creation of a business profile would increase not only active participation but also overall social networking service memberships.

Research by Enterprise Ireland (Fitzsimons & O'Gorman , 2009, p. 17) demonstrated that participation in education or training in relation to entrepreneurship has positive effects on an individual's preparedness and the likelihood of becoming an entrepreneur. Approximately one in four adults (26%) in Ireland has participated in some type of education or training in starting a business. Two in every three early stage entrepreneurs (64%) are not exclusively focused on the Irish market and expect to have some customers outside of Ireland. This is a relatively high export orientation among Irish early stage entrepreneurs compared to their counterparts in the UK (49%), EU (56%) and OECD (54%). These statistics highlight the desire of Irish entrepreneurs to grow internationally.

Social networking services such as LinkedIn can provide Irish entrepreneurs with a cost effective tool that can lower the barriers of international business and make an exporting focus a reality. LinkedIn can provide a safe and trustworthy interaction between Irish entrepreneurs and international partners, without the expense (in time and money) of international travel.

The empirical data from this research suggests that the sample of Irish entrepreneurs have yet to harness the international relationship possibility of using LinkedIn. Only 27% of the immediate connections within the sample were international connections. Three of the entrepreneurs (Entrepreneur 6, 8 and 9) had 0%, 1% and 6% respectively of their connections as international. At a time when the Irish government supports both entrepreneurship and an exporting business model, training in the creation, development and maintenance of international business networking must occur. Social networking services can become the foundation for the connections.

5.6.2 Global business opportunities

The success of the Irish economy is dependent upon the export market. Studies have shown that firms engaged in networking record higher export sales (Perry 1999). Social networking services such as LinkedIn provide global opportunities to Irish entrepreneurs that were difficult to develop and maintain just five years ago. Public policy and marketing of the benefits of social capital are needed to educate Irish entrepreneurs on the real economic value and global opportunities of business networking. For Irish entrepreneurs to expand the use of social networking for global connections there should be an advertising campaign across popular Irish media communicating the benefits of business networking and available support services that are currently offered by business support agencies in

Ireland. The Irish government has embraced the notion that entrepreneurism is an important factor to the national economy. In May 2009 Mary Coughlan, Ireland's Minister for Enterprise, Trade and Employment stated, "Ireland is at heart an entrepreneurial nation. Now more than ever we need to tap into that ability to identify opportunity, assemble resources and create new enterprises. We need to harness the entrepreneurial potential of all the people living within the country" (Fitzsimons & O'Gorman, 2009, p. 9). John McGuiness, the Irish Minister for Trade and Commerce, highlighted the importance of the Irish export market in a speech on March 26, 2009:

> "Over the last number of years, economic growth in Ireland has been driven by domestic demand and not by international competitiveness. As domestic demand has weakened we must look to exports for a sustained economic recovery. Exporters are and will continue to be critical in the achievement of future economic stability and job maintenance and growth in the Irish market." (McGuiness, 2009)

The establishment of new businesses and the support of existing businesses that understand the importance of business networking and social capital need to be a central focus of Irish public policy. It is through these new and existing companies that an economic recovery is possible; a recovery that not only relies upon an internal Irish market, but also one that will support export-focused Irish companies to grow internationally.

5.6.3 Evaluation of existing business networking policy

Despite the existence of government assistance and networking policy interventions in countries such as Ireland, Spain and the United Kingdom dating back almost three decades, there continues to be a lack of evaluation of such interventions (Lynch, 2008). Ireland continues to be a leader in Europe for early stage entrepreneur development (Fitzsimons & O'Gorman, 2009). The advantages of networking accrue to large and small firms alike; however, given the limited resources of small entrepreneurial firms relative to large firms, networking can be seen as much more important to the survival of small businesses (Pyke & Sengenberger, 1992). In a recessionary business environment where publicly funded projects need to show economic value for continued funding, the creation of an effective, systemized evaluation of networking projects is essential.

5.6.3 Modification to conceptual model

After an analysis of the empirical data, it was determined that the relationship between Irish entrepreneurs and the use of technology to form, develop and maintain a business network is not as strong as anticipated. For that reason, a modification to the conceptual model is now presented as an updated descriptive model.

The relationship between the core foundation and technology-based networking is now represented as a dashed line to indicate that this linkage is not as strong as the linkage between business networking, social capital and effects of social capital on entrepreneurs. It is theorized that if this research were to be replicated in the near future, as the usage of technology to form, develop and maintain a business network increases (as the trends in the empirical findings indicate), then the strength of the relationship to using technology within an Irish entrepreneurial network would also strengthen.

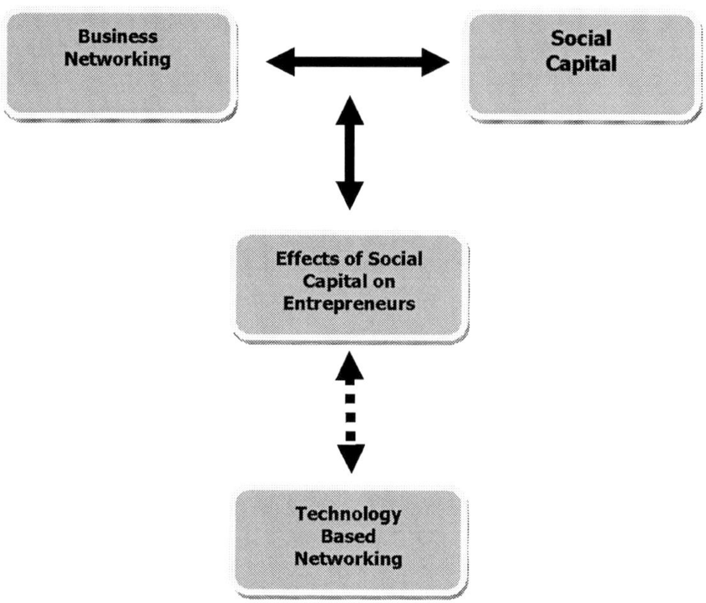

Figure 5.1: Descriptive Model

5.7 Future Research

A number of issues were raised in this research. These issues could be researched further in order to gain a greater insight into the needs of entrepreneurs in Ireland, their motivations, networking practices and the barriers entrepreneurs face. Previous research by Olsen (2008) used a similar interview schedule that would suggest that Norwegian entrepreneurs are more willing to share information using a social networking site such as LinkedIn than are Irish entrepreneurs. Additional research into this area is needed to determine if the type of networking displayed within the research reflects a cultural difference rather than an entrepreneurial phenomenon. One aspect of the report that could be enhanced with future research would be the inclusion of entrepreneurs from different countries to determine how technological advances in each country affect entrepreneurial activity with social capital and the subsequent use of LinkedIn as identified in this research. In addition, a quantitative research project would elicit additional information that would supplement the current literature on this topic.

One question from this research that could be of particular interest is the prevalence of the Irish entrepreneur networking with others outside of Ireland. The initial data suggests that even though LinkedIn has the ability to globalize a potential market, the current trend is that Irish entrepreneurs still do not network outside of Ireland. The following table highlights the total number of connections within the entrepreneur's network with the breakdown of Irish versus non-Irish connections.

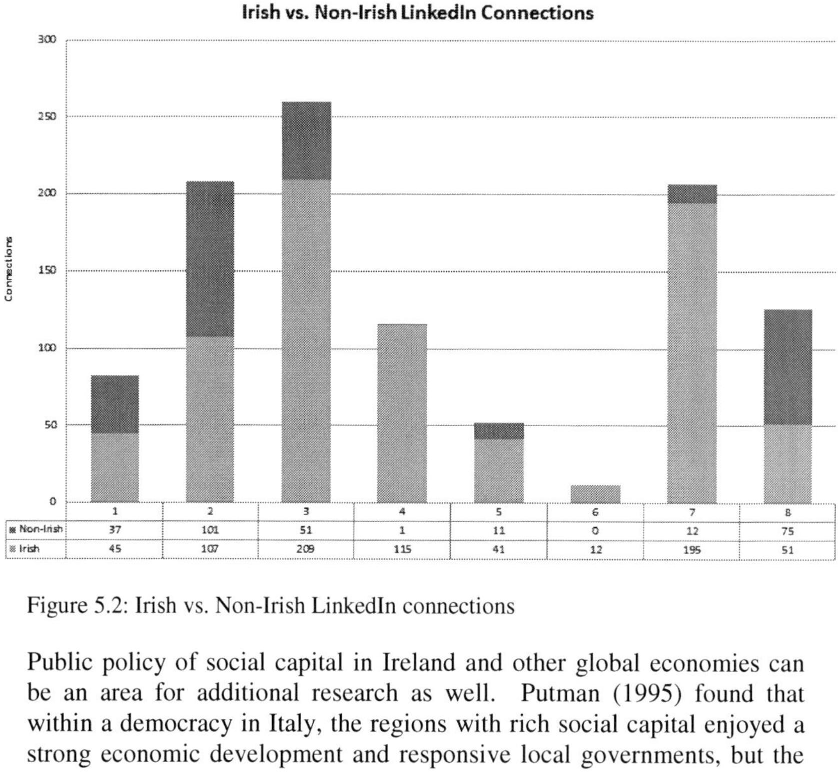

Figure 5.2: Irish vs. Non-Irish LinkedIn connections

Public policy of social capital in Ireland and other global economies can be an area for additional research as well. Putman (1995) found that within a democracy in Italy, the regions with rich social capital enjoyed a strong economic development and responsive local governments, but the regions with poor social capital suffer. Similar communities exist throughout the world and a comparison study would provide an interesting insight into the value of social capital.

5.8 Conclusion

In achieving the primary research objective of the use of technology by Irish entrepreneurs to develop, manage and maintain a business network, the empirical data suggests that while networking is an important aspect of business development, some Irish entrepreneurs still prefer face to face networking over the use of technology. However, the data also suggests that there has been an increase in the use of technology to develop, manage and maintain a business network and that the trend will continue. The research issue was achieved by exploring three research objectives.

Research Objective One explored the perceived benefits of networking. The empirical findings suggested that face to face interactions are important within the Irish culture, but that the use of social networking services such as LinkedIn are growing in popularity. The findings also suggest that for an Irish entrepreneur, the preference is based on personal interaction. Trust and privacy are two important characteristics of an Irish network.

Research Objective Two investigated the formation, maintenance and development of entrepreneurial networks. Entrepreneurs in this research tended to be more passive in their formation of networks and closed in nature. Many of the entrepreneurs found services such as LinkedIn as important tools in the maintenance of the network to stay current with the network, both as a member of the overall network and as the focal point of the network.

Research Objective Three explored the use of technology to manage social capital. It was concluded that while the Irish culture is known as a technology society, the management of social capital remains an offline activity.

In conclusion, the growth of social networking services reported by Boyd and Ellison (2007) indicates that professional networking sites like LinkedIn are expanding at a tremendous rate. This growth and subsequent opportunity will change the way Irish entrepreneurs do business not only in Ireland, but also around the world.

REFERENCES

Adler, Paul S. and Seok-Woo Kwon. (2002) 'Social capital prospects for a new concept', Academy of Management Review, 27(1),17-40.

Aldrich, H. E. and Martinez, M. A. (2001) 'Many are called but few are chosen: An evolutionary perspective for the study of entrepreneurship', Entrepreneurship Theory and Practice, 25(4): 41–56.

Aldrich, H. E. and Zimmer, C. (1986) 'Entrepreneurship through Social Networks', in D. Sexton and R. Smilor (eds.), The Art and Science of Entrepreneurship, 2–23. New York: Ballinger Publishing Company.

Allen, I. and Seaman, C. (2007) 'Likert scales and data analyses', Quality Progress, 40(7), 64.

Amaratunga, D., Baldry, D., Sarshar, M. and Newton, R. (2002) 'Quantitative and qualitative research in the build environment: Application of mixed research approach', Work Study, 51(1), 17-31.

Ancona, D. G. and Caldwell, D.F. (1988) 'Beyond task and maintenance', Group & Organization Studies, 13(4), 468-494.

Anda, B. and Hove, S. (2005) "Conducting semi-structured interviews in empirical software engineering research", Software Metrics, 23-33.

Anderson Analytics. (2008) 'Anderson Analytics', viewed 13 June 2009, <http://www.andersonanalytics.com/>.

Anderson, A. R. and Jack, S. L. (2002) 'The articulation of social capital in entrepreneurial networks: A glue or a lubricant?' Entrepreneurship & Regional Development, 14(3), 193-210.

Anderson, A. R. and Miller, C. (2002) '"Class matters: Human and social Capital in the entrepreneurial process', Journal of Socio-Economics, 32, 17–36.

Baker, W. (2000) Achieving Success Through Social Capital: Tapping the Hidden Resources In Your Personal and Business Networks, First Edition, New York, NY: University of Michigan Business School.

Baron, R. & Shane, S. (2005) Entrepreneurship: A process perspective. Cincinnati, OH: Southwestern Thomson.

Barringer, B. and Ireland, R. (2008) Entrepreneurship - Successfully Launching New Ventures, Second Edition. Pearson Education International.

Baym, N.K., Zhang, Y.B. and Lin, M.C. (2004) 'Social interactions across media', New Media and Society, 6(3), 299-318.

Bergfeld C. (2008) 'LinkedIn Snags Biggest Social Network Growth', Media Industry, viewed 13 June 2009, <http://industry.bnet.com/media/2008/04/23/linkedin-snags-biggest-social-network-growth/trackback/>.

Bergman, E. M. and Fesser, E. J. (eds.) (2000) Industrial and Regional Clusters: Concepts and Comparative Applications. West Virginia University.

Birley, S., Crommie, S. and Myers, A. (1991) 'Entrepreneurial networks: Their emergence in Ireland and overseas', International Small Business Journal, 9(4), 56-74.

Blundel, R. and Smith, D. (2001) 'Business Networks: SMEs and inter-firm collaboration: A review of the research literature with implications for policy', Small Business Services.

Bogdan R. C. & Biklen, S. K. (1998) Qualitative Research for Education: An Introduction to Theory and Methods. Boston: Allyn and Bacon.

Bolton, B. and Thompson, J. (2000) Entrepreneurs: Talent, Temperament and Technique. Oxford: Butterworth-Heinemann.

Boyd, D.M. and Ellison, N.B. (2007) 'Social network sites: Definition, history, and scholarship', Journal of Computer-Mediated Communication, 13 (1), viewed 11 January 2009, <http://jcmc.indiana.edu/vol13/issue1/boyd.ellison.html>.

Bryman, A. and Bell, E. (2007) Business Research Methods, Second Edition, New York: Oxford University Press.

Burns, P. and Dewhurst, J. (1996) Small Business and Entrepreneurship. Basingstoke: Macmillian Press.

Bygrave, W.D. (1989) 'The entrepreneurship paradigm (II): Chaos and catastrophes among quantum jumps?' Entrepreneurship Theory and Practice, 14(4), 730.

Carton, R. B., Hofer, C.W. and Meeks, M.D. (1998) 'The Entrepreneur and Entrepreneurship - Operational Definitions of the Role in Society', In International Council for Small Business. Singapore.

Charmaz, K. (1983) The Grounded Theory Method: An Explication and Interpretation. In Emerson, R.M., ed., Contemporary Field Research: A Book of Readings. Boston: Little, Brown.

—. (2000) Grounded Theory: Objectivist and Contructivist Methods, 2nd Edition, Thousand Oaks, CA: Safe.

Chell, E. and Baines, S. (2000) 'Networking, entrepreneurship and micro-business behaviour', Entrepreneurship and Regional Development, 12(3), 195–215.

Churchill, N.C. and Lewis, V.L. (1986) 'Entrepreneurship research: directions and methods', in Sexton, D. L. and Smilor, R.W., eds., The

Art and Science of Entrepreneurship, Cambridge, MA: Ballinger Publishing Co.

Coleman, J. S., ed. (1990) Foundations of Social Theory, Cambridge, MA: Harvard University Press.

Cooke, P. and Wills, D. (1999) 'Small firms, social capital and the enhancement of business performance through innovation programmes', Small Business Economics, 13, 219-234.

Cope, J., Jack, S. and Rose, M. B. (2007) 'Social capital and entrepreneurship: An introduction', International Small Business Journal, 25(3), 213-219.

Creswell, J.W. (1994) Research Design: Qualitative and Quantitative Approaches. Thousand Oaks, CA: Sage.

Crommie, S. (1994) 'Entrepreneurship: the role of the individual in small business development', IBAR, 15, 62-75.

Curren, J., Jarvis, R., Blackburn, R.A. and Black, S. (1993) 'Networks and small firms: Constructs, methodological strategies and some findings', International Small Business Journal, 11(2), 13-25.

Dana, L.P. (2001) 'The education and training of entrepreneurs in Asia', Education and Training, 43(8/9), 405-414.

Davidsson, P. and Honig, B. (2003) 'The role of social and human capital among Nascent Entrepreneurs', Journal of Business Venturing, 18(4), 301–31.

De Carolis, D. M., Litzky, B. E. and Eddleston, K. A. (2009) 'Why networks enhance the progress of new venture creation: The influence of social capital and cognition', Entrepreneurship: Theory & Practice, 33(2), 527-545.

De Carolis, D.M. and Saparito, P. (2006) 'Social capital, cognition, and entrepreneurial opportunities: A theoretical framework', Entrepreneurship: Theory & Practice, 30(1), 41-56.

Dittmer, R. and McFarland, S. (2008) 151 Quick Ideas to Improve Your People Skills: Career Press.

Dollinger, M.J. (1985) 'Environmental contact and financial performance of the small firm', Journal of Small Business Management ,1, 24-30.

Dosi, G. (1988) 'Sources, procedures, and microeconomic effects of innovation', Journal of Economic Literature, 26 (3), 1120–1171.

Dubini, P. & Aldrich, H. (1991) 'Personal and extended networks are central to the entrepreneurial process', Journal of Business Venturing, 6, 305–313.

Dudwick, N., Kuehnast, K., Nyhan-Jones, V. and Woolcock, M. (2006) Analyzing Social Capital in Context: A Guide to Using Qualitative Methods and Data. World Bank White Paper Stock No. 37260:46.

Eisenhardt, K. M. (1989) 'Building theories from case study research', Academy of Management Review, 14, 532-550.

Ellison, N.B., Steinfield, C. and Lampe, C. (2007) 'The benefits of Facebook "friends": Social capital and college students'?, Journal of Computer-Mediated Communication, viewed 13 June 2009, <http://jcmc.indiana.edu>.

Enterprise Ireland. (2009) 'Enterprise Ireland', <http://www.enterprise-ireland.com>.

Fafchamps, M. and Minten, B. (1999) 'Relationships and traders in Madagascar', Journal of Development Studies, 35(6), 1-35.

Ferrazzi, K. and Raz, T. (2005) Never Eat Alone: And Other Secrets to Success, One Relationship at a Time. Broadway Business.

Ffowcs-Williams, I. (ed.) (2003) 'Policy for inter-firm clustering. A Practitioners Guide', Enhancing the competitiveness of SMEs in the Global Economy: Strategies and Policies, Bologna, Italy.

Field, J. (2003) Social Capital. London: Routledge.

Fitzsimons, P. and O'Gorman C. (2009) IRELAND 2008 GEM NATIONAL REPORT, viewed August 1, 2009, <www.gemconsortium.org/download.asp?fid=895>.

Fraser, M. and Dutta, S. (2008) Throwing Sheep in the Boardroom: How Online Social Networking Will Transform Your Life, Work and World. Wiley.

Flichy, P. (2006) New Media History - Handbook of New Media. London, California and New Delhi: Sage Publications, Ltd.

Garton, L., Haythornthwaite, C. and Wellman, B. (1997) 'Studying online social networks', Journal of Computer-Mediated Communication, 1(3), viewed 28 December 2008, <http://jcmc.indiana.edu/vol3/issue1/garton.html>.

Gill, J. and Johnson, P. (1991) Research Methods for Managers. London: Paul Champman Publishing.

Ghauri, P. and Gronhaug, K. (2005) Research Methods in Business Studies: A Practical Guide. Prentice Hall.

Glaser, B. G. and Strauss, A. L. (1967) The Discovery of Grounded Theory: Strategies for Qualitative Research. Chicago, IL: Aldine.

Granovetter, M. S. (1973) 'The strength of weak ties', The American Journal of Sociology, 78(6), 1360-1380.

Haythornthwaite, C. (2000) 'Online personal networks', New Media and Society, 2(2), 195-226.

Heath, A. (1997) 'The proposal in qualitative research', The Qualitative Report, 3(1), <http://www.nova.edu/ssss/QR/QR3-1/heath.html>.

Hirsch, B. (1981) 'Social Networks and the Coping Process: Creating Personal Communities', Gottlieb, B. (ed.), Social Networks and Social Support, p. 169. Thousand Oaks, CA.

Hof, R. (2008) 'Facebook in a suit: LinkedIn launches applications platform', Business Week, viewed 13 June 2009, <http://www.businessweek.com/the_thread/teachbeat/archives/2008/10/linkedin_launch.html>.

Huggins, R. (2000) 'The success and failure of policy-implanted interfirm network initiatives: Motivations, process and structure', Entrepreneurial and Regional Development, 12, 211–236.

Hynes, B. (2002) Research Methodologies. Limerick: University of Limerick.

Jacobson, D. I. (2005) How to Conduct Research? An Introduction to Social Science Methodology. Kristiansand: Hoyskoleforl.

Johannisson, B., ed. (2000) Networking and entrepreneurial growth. Oxford: Blackwell.

Jones, S. (1999) Doing internet research. California, London and New Delhi: Sage Publications Inc.

Jones, G. (2009) Social networking is being hampered by lack of understanding. viewed September 1, 2009, www.grahamjones.co.uk/blog/social-networking/social-networking-is-being-hampered-by-lack-of-understanding.html.

Kets de Vries, M. F. R. (1977) 'The entrepreneurial personality: A person at the crossroads', Journal of Management Studies, 14(1), 34–57.

Kim, P. H. and Aldrich, H. E. (2005) 'Social capital and entrepreneurship', Foundations and Trends in Entrepreneurship, 1(2), 1–52.

Kirzner, I. M. (1973) Competition and Entrepreneurship. Chicago, IL: University of Chicago.

Lechner, C. and Dowling, M. (2003) 'Firm networks: External relationships as sources of growth and competitiveness of entrepreneurial firms', Entrepreneurship and Regional Development, 15, 1–26.

LinkedIn. (2009) 'LinkedIn', viewed 13 June 2009, <http://www.linkedin.com>.

Low, M.B. and MacMillian, I.C. (1988) 'Entrepreneurship: past research and future challenges', Journal of Management, 14(2), 139-161.

Lynch, N., Lenihan, H., and Hart, M. (2009) 'Developing a framework to evaluate business networks: The case of Ireland's industry-led network initiative', Policy Studies, 30(2), 163-180.

Marshall, C. and Rossman, G.B. (1995) Designing Qualitative Research, 2nd Edition, California: Academic Press.

Miles, M. and Huberman, M. (1984) Qualitative Data Analysis: A Source Book for New Methods. Thousand Oaks, CA: Sage Publications.

Nahapiet, J. and Ghoshal, S. (1997) 'Social capital, intellectual capital and the creation of value in firms', Academy of Management Best Paper Proceedings.

Nardi, B.A., Whittaker, S. and Schwarz, H. (2002) 'NetWORKers and their activity in Intentional Networks', Computer Supported Cooperative Work, 11, 205-242.

Newman, M.E.J. (2003) 'The structure and function of complex networks", SIAM Review, 45(2), 167-256.

Nvivo. (2009) 'Nvivo', viewed 13 June 2009, <www.nvivo.com>.

O'Donnell, A. and Cummins, D. (1999) 'The use of qualitative methods to research networking in SMEs', Qualitative Market Research: An International Journal, 2(2), 82-91.

O'Gorman, C. (1997) Enterprise in Action: An Introduction to Entrepreneurship in an Irish Context. Dublin, Ireland: Oak Tree Press.

Olsen, L. E. (2008) 'Professional Networking Online - A Qualitative Study of LinkedIn Use in Norway', Department of Information Science and Media Studies: University of Bergen.

Perry, M. (1999) 'Small firms and network economies'. London: Routledge.

Putnam, R. D. (1995) 'Bowling alone: America's declining social capital', Journal of Democracy, 6, 65-78.

—. ?ed. (2000) Bowling Alone: The Collapse and Revival of American Community. New York: Simon & Schuster.

Pyke, F. and Sengenberger, W. (1992) Industrial districts and local economic regeneration. Geneva: International Institute of Labour Studies.

Ragin, C., Nagle, J. and White, P., eds. (2003) 'General Guidance for Developing Qualitative Research Projects', Arlington, VA: National Science Foundation.

Remenyi, D., Williams, B., Money, A. and Swartz, E. (2005) Doing Research in Business and Management. London, California and New Delhi: Sage Publications Ltd.

Robson, C. (1993) Real World Research: A Resource for Social Scientists and Practitioner-Researchers. Oxford, UK: Blackwell.

Rogers, E. M. (2003) Diffusion of innovations (5th ed.). New York: Free Press.

Rohmetra, N. (2005) Human Resource Development: Challenges and Opportunities, Anmol Publications PVT.

Sapient Interactive (2009) 'Lack of understanding' hampers social network campaigns', viewed 1 September 2009, <www.netimperative.com/netimperative/news/2009/march/2018lack-of-understanding2019-hampers-social>.

Schumpeter, J. (1947) 'The creative response in economic history', Journal of Economic History, 7, 149-159.

—. ?(1949) 'Economic theory and entrepreneurial history', Journal of Economic History.

Securities and Exchange Commission (2011) 'LinkedIn Form S-1', viewed January 29, 2011 , http://www.sec.gov/Archives/edgar/data/1271024/000119312511016022/ds1.htm>.

Silverman, D. (2006) Interpreting Qualitative Data. London: Sage Publications Ltd.

Strauss, A. and Corbin, J. (1998) Basics of Qualitative Research: Techniques and Procedures for Developing Grounded Theory. Thousand Oaks, CA: Sage Publishing.

Tsai, W. and Ghoshal, S. (1998) 'Social capital and value creation: The role of intrafirm networks', Academy of Management Journal, 4, 464-477.

Vermeiren, J. (2008) How to really use LinkedIn. Ghent, Belgium: Booksurge.

Volery, T. (2004) Handbook of Research on International Entrepreneurship. Cheltenham: Edward Elgar Publishing Limited.

Yin, R. K. (2003) Case Study Research: Design and Methods, 3rd Edition, Thousand Oaks, CA: Sage.

Young, N. (1998) 'The Structure and Substance of African American Entrepreneurial Networks: Some Preliminary Findings', in Reynolds, P.D., Bygrave, W.D., Carter, N.M., Manigart, S., Mason, C.M., Meyer, G.D., and Shaver. K.G. (eds.), Frontiers of Entrepreneurship Research, pp. 118–31, Wellesley, MA: Babson College.

APPENDIX 1

INTERVIEW GUIDE

C1. Are you an entrepreneur? YES NO
C2. How many employees in your current company? (Count yourself as one employee)

1 2-4 5-9 10-24 25-49 50-99 100-249 Over 250

C3. Gender Male Female
C4. Age 20-24 25-29 30-34 35-39 40-44 45-49 50-54 55-59 60-64 65+
C5. Have you ever lived outside of your country of birth for longer than 6 months? Where?

O1. **I am very interested in why you became a member of LinkedIn. (11 SUB QUESTIONS)**

- Education? Career? Conscious or random decision?
- How did you get to know about LinkedIn?
- What version of LinkedIn do you have? Pay/Free? Any reason for this choice?
- Have you been/are you a member of any other social networking services?
    - YES: What kind of services? How are these services compared to LinkedIn?
    - Do you use them often/different?
    - NO: Is there any reason why you're only a member of LinkedIn?
- How long have you used LinkedIn?
- Do you see yourself continuing using the service in the future?
- What types of situations do you see yourself using the service?
- What kind of expectations do you have to professional networking services? Why is this important to you?
- Does LinkedIn fulfil your expectations? Examples?
- What do you think is positive about the service?
- Is there anything negative about it?

O2. Do you get in touch with new people?
18 SUB QUESTIONS

- Do you get new contacts? How? Examples?
- Who do you contact? Have you ever contacted any unknown people?
- How do you contact them?
- What kind of relationship do you have to these contacts now?
- Is there anyone you haven't gotten a reply from?
- Who contacts you? Have you been contacted by any unknown people?
- How do they contact you?
- What kind of relationship do you have with them now?
- Is there anyone you haven't answered?
- What kind of people do you get in touch with? Entrepreneurs? Projects? Education and career? How many?
- What use is the LinkedIn network to you? Examples?
- OR/AND does it help to maintain existing relationships? Who? How? Examples?
    - Have you found any old acquaintances through LinkedIn? Gotten back in touch? Examples?
    - Have you consciously searched for old acquaintances? Example?
    - Have any old acquaintances found you? Example?
    - Have any of the relationships evolved with the help of LinkedIn? How? Who?
    - Is there anyone you are in contact with out of the work-context? Have you made any new friends? Examples?
- Have you deleted any contacts? Who? Why?

03. Does LinkedIn organize your network?
4 SUB QUESTIONS

- Do you manage to keep in control of all of your contacts?
- How many contacts do you have? Do you know who all of them are?
    - How many of your contacts do you know?
    - How did the ones you don't know wind up in your contact list?
    - Why do you keep them in your contact list?
- Has anything become easier since you've started using the LinkedIn network?

What?

- Is there anything you would like to change about the LinkedIn network? What?

O4. How do you use your contacts?
12 SUB QUESTIONS

- How often do you log on to LinkedIn? Time?
- What do you think about spending time on networks like LinkedIn?
- Do you use your existing contacts on LinkedIn? How? Examples?
- What is your approach?
- When do you use your contacts? To what?
- Have you ever gotten rejected/not gotten an answer? Example?
- Have you ever sent an InMail? Used an introduction? Example/Wanted to?
- What do you think about these functions?
- What kind of relationship do you have with your contacts?
    - o Strong/weak ties? Example?
    - o Professionals/friends? What do you have more of? Who do you contact the most?
- Have any of the relationships evolved? Has LinkedIn played a part in this? Example?

05. All human beings have a social network. What does this social network mean to you?
9 SUB QUESTIONS

- Professional network vs. personal-networks? Are they separated? What is the difference? Different in use? Exceptions? Do they blend?
- Do you use your personal-network in job-contexts? Example?
- How do you keep in touch with people in your personal network? Tools?
- Who do you have contact with? Anyone you don't have contact with that you wish you had?
- How do you regard network-building? Positive/negative? Why? Examples?
- What is it about network-building that is important to you?
- What part of your personal network does LinkedIn represent? Example?

- Do you feel it is important to have an online network like LinkedIn? What is it that makes it/doesn't make it important? In what situations has it been important to you? Examples?
- What does this kind of network mean to you? Do you think anything would be different without it? Examples?

O6. How do you experience LinkedIn with regard to establishing, maintaining and developing relations?
2 SUB QUESTIONS

- Does it work?
- Just an address book or is it more than that? What do you think makes it/doesn't make it something else?

C6. What are the business reasons you use social networking services?
(1 Strongly Agree - 2 Agree – 3 Neutral – 4 Disagree – 5 Strongly DisagreeN/A)

Career opportunities
New ventures
Expertise requests
Stay connected
Future business opportunities
Partnership opportunities
Personal networking with connections
Research
Sales prospecting
Other

C7. How do you communicate with your connections?
(1 Work Use Only – 2 Personal Use Only – 3 Both Work and Personal N/A)

Phone call
Mail letter
Personal Email
Group Email
Press releases
Online newsletter
Blog
Website
LinkedIn
Facebook

C8. Some people use one main system to keep their list of connections, some people have multiple lists. Some are electronic, some are paper based. Where do you keep your list of connections (mark all that apply)?

Pen and Paper Address Book
Contact Manager program (like Outlook, address book, etc)
Online address book
LinkedIn

C9. Do you keep separate lists for business connections and personal connections?

C10. How many TOTAL connections do you have?

C11. How often do you use the following?
(1 Many times per day - 2 Once per day – 3 Weekly – 4 Monthly - 5 Yearly – 6 Never)

Email
LinkedIn
Facebook
Bebo
MySpace
Friendster
Twitter
Blog posts
Telephone calls
Postal mail

C12. How would you identify yourself (both online and offline)

A loner
Have a few close friends
Friendly to those that know me
Always looking to make new friends and connections

C13. Please rate your agreement with the following statements
(1 Strongly Agree – 2 Agree - 3 Neutral – 4 Disagree – 5 Strongly Disagree - N/A)

The people I am connected with through my social networks are people I would consider "true friends"

I have become friends with people I would otherwise not know through my social networks

I feel like I know my connections better because of LinkedIn.

I would have lost contact with people had it not been for my social networking.
I have reconnected with people who are important to me through social networking.
I have reconnected with people through social networking, but they are not that important to me.
I make offline plans with people through social networks.

C14. What phrase do you most agree with regarding your use of online social networking?

I'd rather social network offline
I am not interested in online social networking
It is a means to an end
I would spend more time using online social networking if I could
I spend too much time using online social networking

C15. Which statement represents you regarding technology?

I am usually one of the first to try out a new service
I usually jump into a new service after other have tried it first
I tend to wait until a majority of my friends are involved
I only become involved when I have to

C16. On average, how many hours per week do you spend acquiring new business contacts?

C17. On average, how many hours per week do you spend maintaining existing business contacts?

C18. On average, how many times per week do you communicate with potential business contacts?

C19. On average, how many times per week do you communicate with actual business contacts?

C20. Do you connect more or less with your connections than compared to 5 years ago?

I connect more now than 5 years ago
I connect less now than 5 years ago

C21. Do you use technology (email, blog, websites, LinkedIn, Facebook, etc). more or less than 5 years ago?

More

Less

C22. Has the use of technology made communications with your connections more or less efficient than 5 years ago?

C23. What percentage of your success do you attribute to how you manage your connections?

APPENDIX 2

LINKEDIN FEATURES

LinkedIn is an ever expanding collection of different features designed for presenting profiles, expanding networks and member interaction (Olsen, 2008). To explain the features in this paper, LinkedIn will be divided into four main discussion categories: create, connect, activate and applicate.

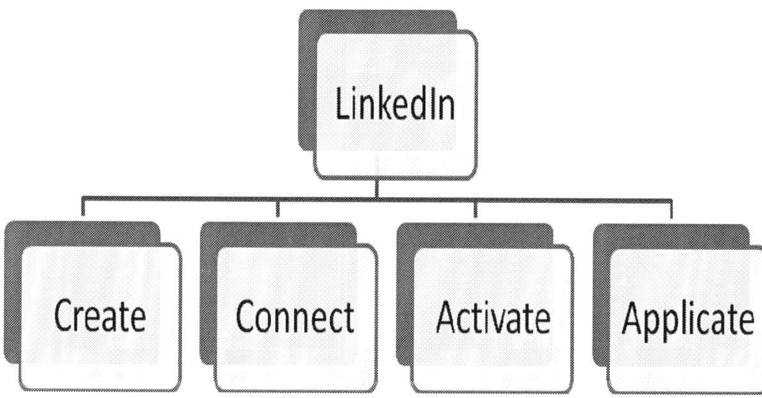

Create

The first phase of LinkedIn usage is the creation of a member profile. In many ways, the profile is the hub and the most important feature of LinkedIn. It is from the profile page that all other aspects of the service are created. A potential member of LinkedIn creates a basic profile containing minimal demographic information that can include but is not limited to name, email address, location, work status, title and industry. The member also has the option to upload their own picture for their profile. Once sign-in details are established with LinkedIn, the member can then add pertinent information to their profile page. In many ways, the profile page is a member's online resume that can include similar information including a general summary, current work experience, past work experience, educational background, recommendations, connections and websites.

Overview

As is often said, "The first impression is often the most important". A member's LinkedIn overview allows a member to control what information can be seen on their profile and allows a member to showcase their skills and talents so that the right people and opportunities find you (LinkedIn, 2009). A LinkedIn profile is discoverable through millions of search engines on the internet and on LinkedIn (LinkedIn, 2009).

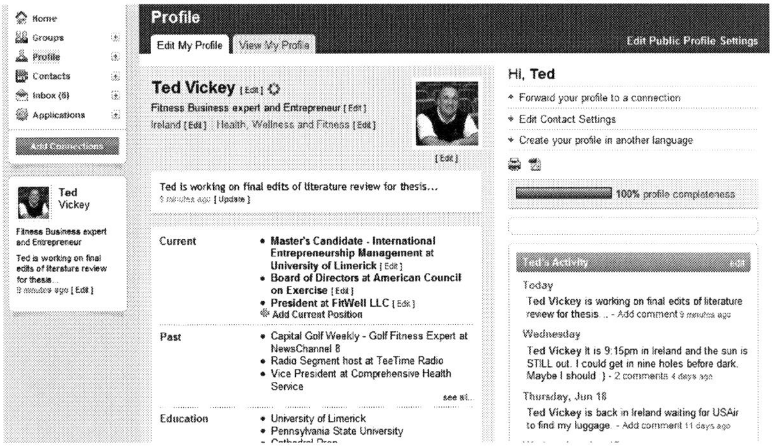

A member profile has two different views reachable through clickable tabs in this section:

- View My Profile: see profile as network does
- Edit My Profile: edit the different elements of profile

Snapshot

The snapshot features an overview of a member's name, location, current title, past positions, education, recommendations and links to their websites. When viewing other profiles, a member will see a list of icons and options to the right of the snapshot. LinkedIn allows a member to control which parts of their profile will be visible to search engine users. Members can make their profile completely private (it will not come up with web searches), turn it on to full-view, or customize the display of individual elements. A member can also create a "Vanity URL" for their public profile, giving them a custom web address to include on business cards, email signatures, etc. for linking to and promoting their profile. Other aspects of the snapshot include:

- Send a message: Allows a member to send a message to the user if connected, or an inMail if you are not connected
- Add to Network: Adds the user to member's network
- Recommend: Write a recommendation for connection
- Forward profile: Allows members to introduce connections to others within LinkedIn
- Search for references: Search through the member's companies for potential references
- One Click Reference: Conduct a quick reference check on the member currently viewing
- Print: Prints the currently viewed profile
- PDF: Saves a PDF Version of the currently viewed profile
- Download vCard: Download connections details into desktop address book

Status

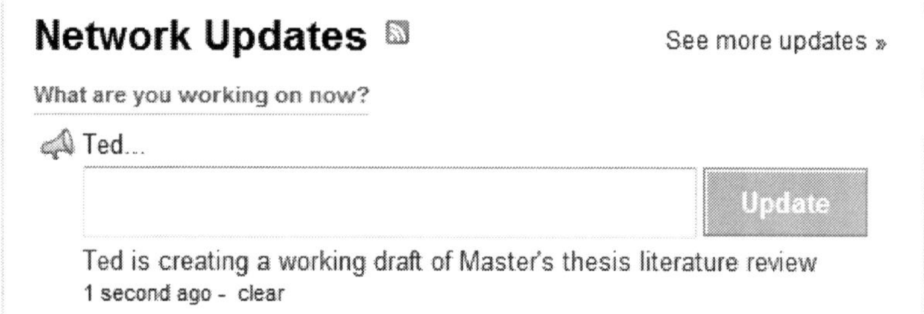

The status message allows a member to share professional updates with their network. By displaying things like what they are currently working on, what assistance might be needed and where they are planning on travelling to, etc., a member can invite their network to help with advice and recommendations.

Summary

The summary section allows a member to provide their professional experience and goals, thus allowing other users to quickly learn about their background and interests. The specialties field allows a member to list their areas of expertise that will help potential employers and partners find them when they are looking for a specific skill-set or knowledge-base.

Summary

Founder and President of FitWell LLC. FitWell is a fitness management consulting company specializing in operations, design consulting and professional development to the fitness industry, government agencies, Fortune 1000 companies and the golf industry.

In addition to his FitWell duties, member of the Board of Directors for the American Council on Exercise, the largest non-profit accredited certification organization in the fitness industry.

From 1994 - 2005 was the Executive Director of the White House Athletic Center, the fitness center serving the fitness, wellness and health promotion needs of the staff at the Executive Office of the President in Washington, DC under the Bush, Clinton and Bush administrations.

Distinguished career as a senior-level Business Executive, author and presenter on many topics including the integration of technology and wellness and management consultant.

Specialties

* Visionary Leadership
* Revenue Growth
* Operation Management
* Strategic Alliances
* Team Building
* Technology
* Change Management
* Corporate Development
* Contract Negotiations
* Procurement

Experience

The experience section is sorted in chronological order and includes a member's professional experiences along with any recommendations they may have received. This area was designed for position descriptions that briefly explain the experience, the member's main responsibilities and accomplishments for easy viewing.

President
FitWell LLC
Health, Wellness and Fitness industry
May 1994 – Present (15 years 2 months)

FitWell is a fitness management consulting company specializing in operations, design consulting and professional development to the fitness industry, government agencies, Fortune 1000 companies and the golf industry.

Ted has 9 recommendations (6 co-workers, 3 partners) including:

- 1st Randy Friedman [Randy@golfmindpower.com], *President, Golf Mind Power LLC*
- 1st Vicky Likens, *Owner, Virtually The Best, Ltd.*

Education

The education section is sorted in chronological order displaying a member's education background highlighting their degree(s), associated activities and honours. Including a detailed description in this area will allow former classmates and educational partners to connect with individual members.

Education

University of Limerick
MS, International Entrepreneurship Management
2008 – 2009

Pennsylvania State University
BS
1987 – 1991

Internship - White House Athletic Center under Bush Administration - 1991

Activities and Societies: Member - Water Polo Team 1987 - 1991

Member - Moosehouse Society 1987 - 1990

Cathedral Prep
1983 – 1987

Additional information

The additional information section of a member profile allows the member to provide additional insight into their professional qualifications by providing the following:

- Websites: link to a personal blog, company website, etc.,
- Interests: list the things that they enjoy doing, learning about, etc.,
- Groups and Associations: either list professional organizations or display badges of LinkedIn groups that they are a part of,
- Honours and Awards.

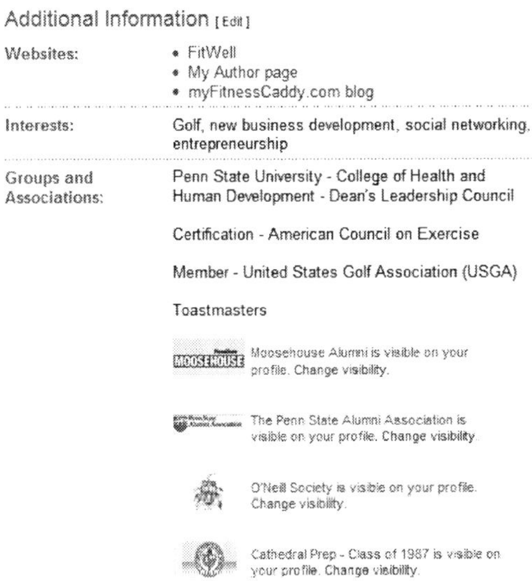

Recommendations

The recommendation section allows a member illustrate their achievements, project credibility and additional information. The recommendations are from other members of LinkedIn that the member is connected to and have had some sort of professional relationship with in the past.

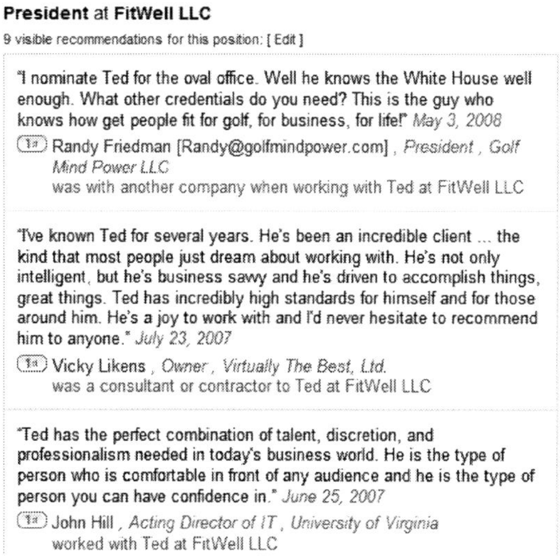

President at **FitWell LLC**

9 visible recommendations for this position: [Edit]

"I nominate Ted for the oval office. Well he knows the White House well enough. What other credentials do you need? This is the guy who knows how get people fit for golf, for business, for life!" *May 3, 2008*

(1st) Randy Friedman [Randy@golfmindpower.com] , *President , Golf Mind Power LLC*
was with another company when working with Ted at FitWell LLC

"I've known Ted for several years. He's been an incredible client ... the kind that most people just dream about working with. He's not only intelligent, but he's business savvy and he's driven to accomplish things, great things. Ted has incredibly high standards for himself and for those around him. He's a joy to work with and I'd never hesitate to recommend him to anyone." *July 23, 2007*

(1st) Vicky Likens , *Owner , Virtually The Best, Ltd.*
was a consultant or contractor to Ted at FitWell LLC

"Ted has the perfect combination of talent, discretion, and professionalism needed in today's business world. He is the type of person who is comfortable in front of any audience and he is the type of person you can have confidence in." *June 25, 2007*

(1st) John Hill , *Acting Director of IT , University of Virginia*
worked with Ted at FitWell LLC

Connect

To make one's membership on LinkedIn as successful as possible, one must connect to other members. It is the connections and the desire for professional interaction that create the online community that is LinkedIn. In theory, the more connections a member has, the bigger that member's network and thus the more potential opportunities (Olsen, 2008). For one member to view another member's contact list, that member must be a 1st connection. When viewing another member's profile it is possible to see how many and to whom that member is connect to, including their 2nd and 3rd degree.

Through the Network Statistic feature, a member can see how many 1st, 2nd and 3rd degree connections are available in their network. In addition, it is possible to view the three top locations and industries in one's member network.

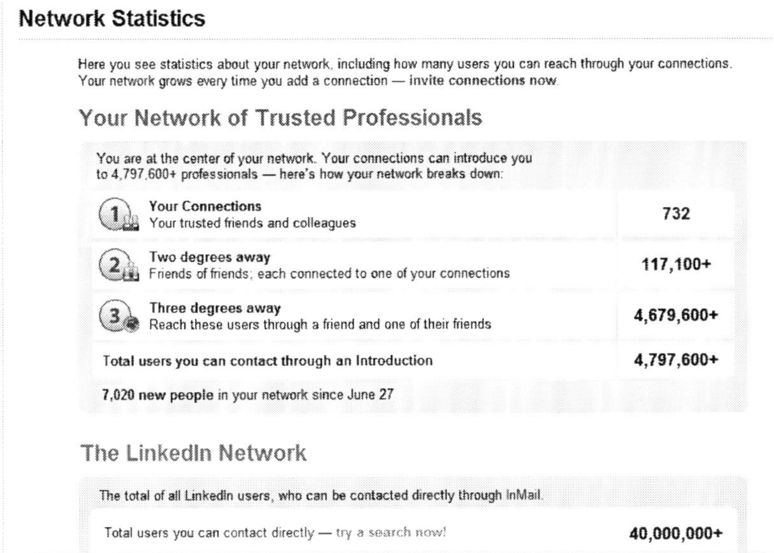

In addition to strengthening one's network and expanding opportunities, LinkedIn also provides updates related to the member's existing network. Through the feature Network Updates, members can view updates with their 1st degree connections, and in so doing, stay updated on their professional lives. When one of their connections adds another connection, makes an update to his/her profile, asks or answers a question, or makes a change to their profile, these changes will be available to their complete LinkedIn network on their overview page. In addition, members can subscribe to a weekly email of network changes. While there is no limit to the number of connections one can have, once a member passes 500 1st degree connections, their profile status reflects 500+ notation rather than actual 1st degree connections.

Activate

LinkedIn provides their membership with the opportunity to connect with other members of their network. The service provides a number of tools with regard to the management of one's network.

Member dashboard

A member's LinkedIn homepage, also known as the member dashboard, provides a member with a status overview of their network, including related news, jobs and answers. This feature includes:

- Individual messages and network updates from colleagues and connections
- News about a member's company, their competitors and industry
- Updates of potential jobs, questions and answers that match a member's interests

Inbox

The inbox is the control panel for all of member LinkedIn user interactions, including messages, introductions and connection requests.

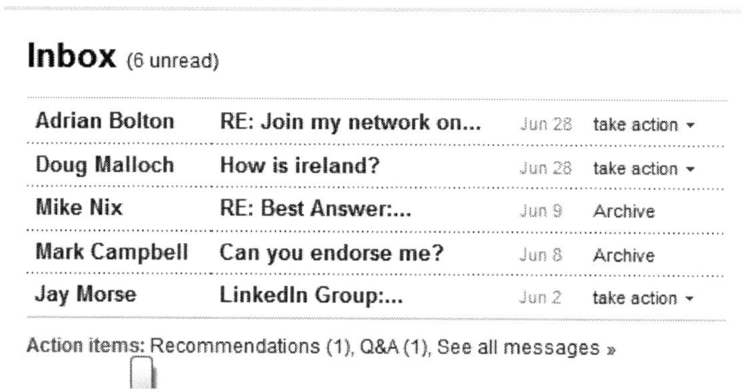

News

Part of the power of one's network is the ability to share and discuss important news that matters to the network. LinkedIn News features a customized news feed for connections. The information is divided into four categories:

- Most Discussed: the articles that are the most popular among people in a member's company,
- Company: the articles about the member's company,

- Other Companies: the articles about the companies that are similar to the member,
- Industry: the articles about the member's industry.

Clicking on the article opens it in a new window. In addition to the article information, there is a 'discuss' link next to each article allowing the member to comment and engage in a discussion about the article with other members of their network.

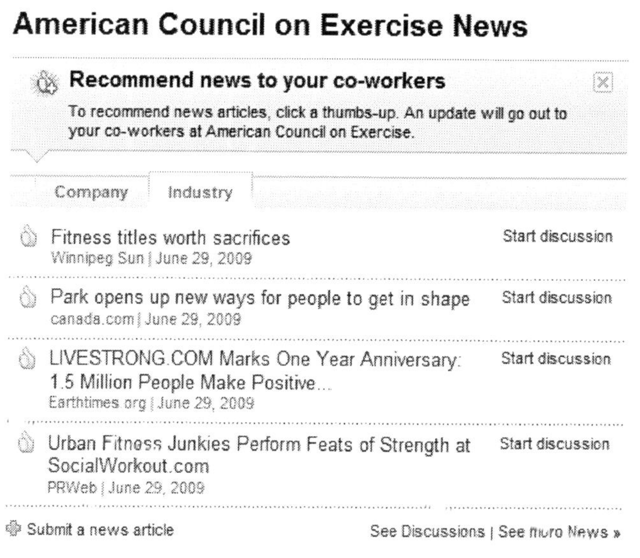

Network Updates

Sorted in chronological order, the Network Update features the latest activities of a member's connections. These activities include, but are not limited to, their current status, groups recently joined, questions asked and answered, and who within the network the member has recently connected to.

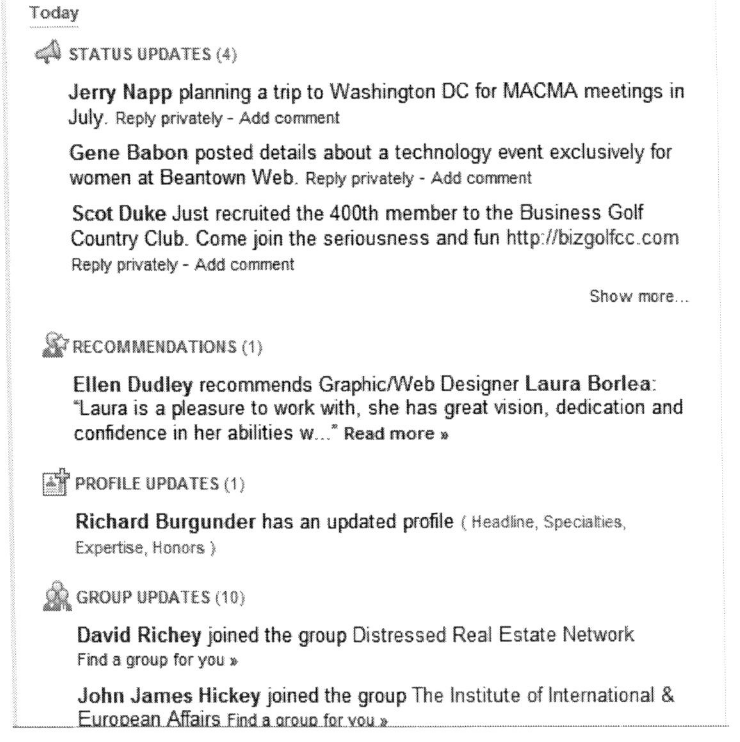

Questions and Answers

The Questions and Answers section of a member's profile allows a member to showcase their knowledge and interests by asking or responding to a LinkedIn member question. The member can control which questions and answers are linked to their profile.

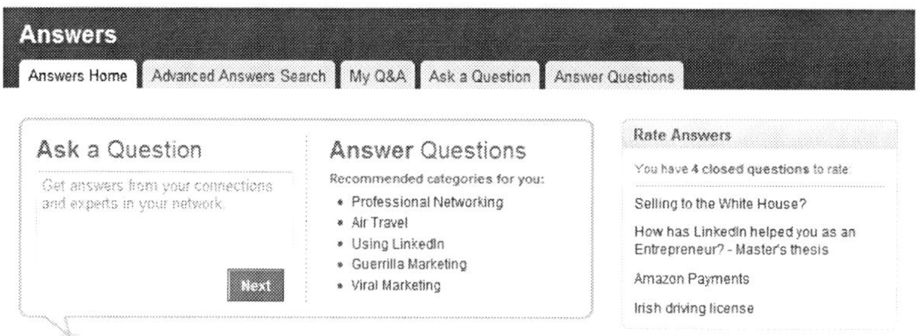

Groups

LinkedIn Groups allows members to find and join communities of professionals based on common interest, experience, affiliation and goals. The service also allows group organizations to extend their brand's reach and strengthen the brand with existing users by providing additional value through LinkedIn's features. Members can easily find a group of interest (Alumni, Corporate, Non-Profit, Corporate, etc) and can join the group by clicking on the "Join Group" link to request to join the group. Membership to a group may be subject to review by a group manager. A list of a member's groups can be found on their dashboard, allowing access to each of their groups and the ability to partake in private discussions. Once a member of a group, a member can view additional members of the group by searching for name, company, or other keywords such as specific areas of expertise. This allows a member to find experts and utilize talent from within their network.

LinkedIn Groups allow members to communicate with their group or organization online. This allows for discussions of issues that are of interest to the entire group.

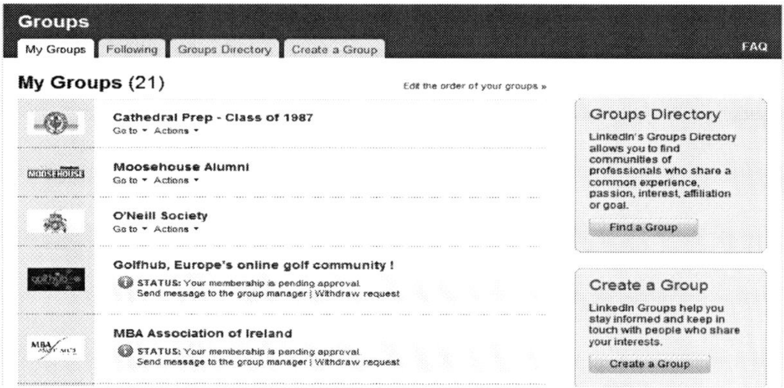

As a member of a particular group, the member can control their contact and privacy settings for each Group. In addition, a member can elect to display the group logo on their profile, change their privacy settings for network updates, and also decide how they want group members to be able to communicate with them.

An additional feature of groups is the "Digest Email" option which allows members to receive updates by e-mail from their group(s).

Applicate

LinkedIn's Intelligent Applications, or InApps, is aimed squarely at the professionals that the business networking service caters to. In a 2009 Business Week interview, Jamie Templeton, LinkedIn's Vice President of platform products, was quoted as saying, "Our audience is a professional audience, it's not the typical social network audience" (Hof, 2008). More than a year after Facebook introduced their own suite of applications, LinkedIn announced its own platform. At the time of the writing of this research, LinkedIn offered nine applications including:

Reading List by Amazon

The Amazon Reading List is a fully integrated application that allows LinkedIn members to share the books they are reading with other LinkedIn members. Professionals can discover what they should be reading by following updates from their connections, people in their industry, or other LinkedIn members of professional interest to them.

Box File Collaboration

The Box.net File Collaboration application helps LinkedIn members manage important files online. The application lets LinkedIn members share content on their profile, collaborate and exchange documents with connections on LinkedIn. In addition to providing free storage and collaboration features, key documents can also be featured directly on a member's profile – a perfect way to showcase recent work, past deals, or a portfolio.

My Travel by Tripit

My Travel shows LinkedIn members where their entire professional network is travelling to and when connections will be in the same city. The My Travel application allows members to easily meet up at the next industry event or re-connect with old friends. The Tripit application is being sponsored by Courtyard at Marriott.

Google Presentations

Google presentations allows LinkedIn members to embed a presentation on their profile to showcase a recent talk or presentation, or display a visual portfolio of professional accomplishments in an easy-to-use click thru format on a LinkedIn profile.

WordPress

The WordPress application allows LinkedIn members to sync WordPress blog posts with their LinkedIn profile in order to share their posts with their connections.

Slideshare

Slideshare allows LinkedIn members to share presentations with colleagues and connections on LinkedIn, and find experts for certain industries and topics who also have presentations to share. Slideshare offers an opportunity for professional branding by allowing members to embed presentations into LinkedIn profiles to feature their portfolio and work.

Blog Link by Six Apart

Blog Link automatically pulls in the latest blog posts from the connections in a LinkedIn member's network so relevant up-to-date information will always be featured in the network updates.

Huddle Workspaces

Huddle gives LinkedIn members private, secure online workspaces packed with simple yet powerful project, collaboration and sharing tools for working with connections.

Company Buzz by LinkedIn

The Company Buzz application allows members to track what is said about their company on Twitter. The application is a filter for Twitter conversations based on search terms and can be customized by members, allowing them to see who is talking about their company and products. The application shows tweets, trends and top key words.

APPENDIX 3

LINKEDIN STATISTICS

According to a recent Anderson Analytics survey, the following is reported regarding LinkedIn users:

- Most users connect to people they know, including those they have met only over the phone.
- Users like the professional and business oriented look and feel of LinkedIn compared to other SNS.
- Users tend to be more senior (56% are "individual contributors", 16% are management level and 28% are director/VP level or above).
- The majority (66%) are decision makers or have influence in the purchase decisions at their companies (decision makers also tend to be more active on LinkedIn).
- The greater the number of connections the greater the likelihood of higher personal income. Those with personal incomes between $200K-$350K were seven times more likely than others to have over 150 connections.

APPENDIX 4

NORWAY RESEARCH STUDY ON LINKEDIN

The research questions used in this study were based on a Norwegian study by Olsen in 2008. The interview guide from the Norway study is listed below.

Interview guide

BEFORE THE INTERVIEW

Ask the informant to present him/herself

Explain why I want to talk to him/her

- Master's thesis. I want to examine how LinkedIn is used and the type of relations that are created, maintained and developed through the LinkedIn network.

Inform about the length of the interview

- It will take about an hour. Is it ok if we use more time, if needed?

Inform about anonymity

- Pass out description of the study and get signature

THE INTERVIEW

I am very interested in why you became a member of LinkedIn.

- Education? Career? Conscious or random decision?
- How did you get to know about LinkedIn?
- What version of LinkedIn do you have? Pay/Free? Any reason for this choice?
- Have you been/are you a member of any other social networking services?

- o YES: What kind of services? How are these services compared to LinkedIn?
- o Do you use them often/different?
- o NO: Is there any reason why you're only a member of LinkedIn?

- How long have you used LinkedIn?
- Do you see yourself continuing using the service in the future?
- What types of situations do you see yourself using the service?
- What kind of expectations do you have to professional networking services?
- Why is this important to you?
- Does LinkedIn fulfil your expectations? Examples?
- What do you think is positive about the service?
- Is there anything negative about it?

Do you get in touch with new people?

- Do you get new contacts? How? Examples?
- Who do you contact? Have you ever contacted any unknown people? Examples?
- How do you contact them?
- What kind of relationship do you have to these contacts now?
- Is there anyone you haven't gotten a reply from?
- Who contacts you? Have you been contacted by any unknown people? Examples?
    - o How do they contact you?
    - o What kind of relationship do you have with them now?
    - o Is there anyone you haven't answered?
- What kind of people do you get in touch with?
- Entrepreneurs? Projects? Education and career? How many?
- What use is the LinkedIn network to you? Examples?
    - o OR/AND does it help to maintain existing relationships? Who? How? Examples?
- Have you found any old acquaintances through LinkedIn? Gotten back in touch?
- Have you consciously searched for old acquaintances? Example?
- Have any old acquaintances found you? Example?
- Have any of the relationships evolved with the help of LinkedIn? How? Who?
- Is there anyone you are in contact with out of the work-context? Have you made any new friends? Examples?
- Have you deleted any contacts? Who? Why?

Does LinkedIn organize your network?

- Do you manage to keep in control of all of your contacts?
- How many contacts do you have? Do you know who all of them are?
- How many of your contacts do you know?
- How did the ones you don't know wind up in your contact list?
- Why do you keep them in your contact list?
- Has anything become easier since you've started using the LinkedIn network?
- Is there anything you would like to change about the LinkedIn network? What?

How do you use your contacts?

- How often do you log on to LinkedIn? Time?
- What do you think about spending time on networks like LinkedIn?
- Do you use your existing contacts on LinkedIn? How? Examples?
- What is your approach?
- When do you use your contacts? To what?
- Have you ever gotten rejected/not gotten an answer? Example?
- Have you ever sent an InMail? Used an introduction? Example/Wanted to?
- What do you think about these functions?
- What kind of relationship do you have with your contacts?
    - Strong/weak ties? Example?
    - Professionals/friends?
    - What do you have more of?
    - Who do you contact the most?
- Have any of the relationships evolved? Has LinkedIn played a part in this? Example?

All human beings have a social network. What does this social network mean to you?

- Professional network vs. personal-networks?
    - Are they separated?
    - What is the difference?
    - Different in use?
    - Exceptions?
    - Do they blend?

- Do you use your personal-network in job-contexts? Example?
- How do you keep in touch with people in your personal network? Tools?
- Who do you have contact with?
- Anyone you don't have contact with that you wish you had?
- How do you regard network-building? Positive/negative? Why? Examples?
- What is it about network-building that is important to you?
- What part of your personal network does LinkedIn represent? Example?
- Do you feel it is important to have an online network like LinkedIn?
    - What is it that makes it/doesn't make it important?
    - In what situations has it been important to you? Examples?
- What does this kind of network mean to you?
- Do you think anything would be different without it? Examples?

- **How do you experience LinkedIn with regard to establishing, maintaining and developing relations? Does it work?**

    - Just an address book or is it more than that? What do you think makes it/doesn't make it something else?

Is there anything you would like to add?
AFTER THE INTERVIEW

Say thanks for the interview.

Ask if it is OK that I get in touch if anything is unclear.